Smart Choices

Smart Choices

A Woman's Guide to Returning to School

Anne Bianchi

Peterson's Guides
Princeton, New Jersey

Library of Congress Cataloging-in-Publication Data

Bianchi, Anne, 1948–
     Smart choices : a woman's guide to returning to school / Anne Bianchi.
       p. cm.
     Includes bibliographical references.
     ISBN 0-87866-989-2
     1. Women—Education (Higher)—United States—Hand-books, manuals, etc. 2. Women college students—United States—Handbooks, manuals, etc. 3. College, Choice of—United States—Handbooks, manuals, etc. 4. College student orientation—United States—Handbooks, manuals, etc.
I. Title.
LC1756.B45 1990
378.1'9822—dc20
                                       90-38217
                                        CIP

Composition and design by Peterson's Guides

Printed in the United States of America

10 9 8 7 6 5 4 3 2 1

Contents

(continued)

Preface

In April of 1988, I was asked to do an article for *Essence* magazine about women who had decided to go back to school. "Give us the numbers and a few quick profiles of women who have actually taken the plunge," said my editor, herself a reentry student.

The article was to be only four pages long, so I envisioned one day of research and another to do the actual writing. What I found, however, was that little had been written on the topic, except for one or two regionally specific articles and a number of very old textbooks. What I also found was that, contrary to my feeling that I'd be writing about a tiny group of people concentrated mainly in big cities, reentry students represented 55 percent of the total student enrollment nationwide. In fact, I was told, by 1990 female "returners" would be the largest group on campus.

Then I started interviewing women who had already gone through a semester or two, and I always heard the same story: "I wish I'd had some kind of book to tell me things like how to choose a school, how to get financial aid, and what problems to expect."

That's when I decided to write *Smart Choices*.

Since then, I've talked to many people who are in the initial stages of making the decision to return to school or who know somebody in that situation. "Let me know when it comes out," they always say. "Sounds like it would be really helpful."

Is it? Well, I won't really know till people start reading it and give me some feedback. I do, however, know one person it has helped already—me! Having switched careers at the age of 38 (from psychologist to writer), I've recently decided to go back to school for an M.F.A. in creative writing. This past spring, I filed for financial aid using the sources listed in this book.

I'll let you know how it turns out.

Anne Bianchi
August 1990

Chapter

1

The Reentry Woman

Every Sunday afternoon, Linda Belfato spends 2 or 3 hours preparing big panfuls of food that she freezes into smaller portions and labels for each day of the week. Then she packs up her weekend bag and waits for her ride back to the university where she is an in-residence undergraduate. "My husband wants to know why I'm not being rushed by any sororities," she says.

For this 47-year-old mother of three, getting a degree is the fulfillment of a dream that goes back to her elementary school days as a straight A student on Chicago's Southside. Linda grew up in a large Italian-Catholic family that, she says, constantly stressed the value of a good education above everything else. "Both my parents knew it was the only chance any of us had to escape the poverty of our neighborhood."

But by the time Linda graduated from high school, two brothers were already in college, and she was told there wasn't enough money to go around. Instead, Linda went to secretarial school. This was financed by her accountant uncle, who thought that, at the very least, she should have some kind of business training. Right after graduation, though, she got married, and her first child was born within a year.

Mark was followed by two other children in quick succession, and, for the next ten years, Linda's only educational option was to take a few evening courses at the local community college whenever she had the time. When her youngest boy started first grade, she enrolled as a part-time student, taking courses in psychology.

"What I remember most about that experience," she says, "was this constant feeling of frustration. Most of my classmates had enough time to read every book on the suggested reading list, and I'd be lucky if I could get through one."

In the spring of 1986, Linda attended her oldest son's college graduation. "He was the valedictorian," she says, "and his speech had to do with the importance of lifelong learning. Just as he was almost finished, I saw him look in my direction.

"'I know,' he said, 'that many parents here are like my mom, that you've put your own educations on hold so that we could get ours. Well, thanks to you and all the sacrifices you made, we're done. Now it's your turn. Go for it.'"

Two months later, Linda entered the university as a full-time undergraduate, carrying 64 credits. This spring she will graduate with a Bachelor of Science in psychology. "I want to go on for graduate work," she says, "then maybe work with abused children or do some kind of family counseling. For my last birthday, my daughter bought me a briefcase. She said if I'm going to start a new life as a professional woman, I might as well look like one."

The Changing Student Population

Twenty years ago, Linda's classmates might have written home about her, "There's this woman in my math class who's old enough to be my mother. . . ." Twenty years ago, however, fewer than 18 percent of the work force were women. Even fewer were single mothers. And college lecture halls like those at the University of Michigan, which at that time held 300 students (with closed-circuit television for the ones in the back rows), were still being filled to capacity by what seemed like a never-ending supply of baby boomers.

"Everything has changed," says John Jordan, Dean of Northeastern University's Part-Time Division. "Today's reality is that colleges are hurting—badly—due to the decrease in the number of 18-year-olds. My own opinion is that if we want to continue to stay in business, we'd better start turning our attention to the adult learner, especially women."

For the most part, colleges have already heeded Jordan's warning. Studies show that women over the age of 25 currently account for one third of all college students. In fact, in the last ten years, their numbers have increased by 75 percent; this is in marked contrast to the less than 15 percent growth in numbers of the traditional 18- to 22-year-olds. (The fastest-growing age group on campus, by the way, is currently the one labeled "women over 65.") By the year 2000, adult women are projected to constitute the majority student presence, whether in a college classroom, a vocational school, a corporate-sponsored course of study, or a union-sponsored program.

In addition, most studies show that while the immediate triggers producing the decision to go back to school are different for each woman (divorce, career change, empty-nest syndrome, etc.), the overall reason is the same in all cases: major life transition.

"Until recently," says Carol Aslanian, Director of the Office of Adult Learning Services for the College Board, "the typical life sequence was remarkably simple and uniform. Almost everyone went to school at age 6, took at one long sitting all the formal education he or she would ever get, moved directly from that to a 'lifetime job' in either marketplace or home, and then retired at age 65 to rust. The three transition points came abruptly and passed quickly. The passages, accepted as functions of age and as beyond individual control, were considered so automatic that little or no responsibility for handling them developed. This worked well as far as meeting the needs of a burgeoning economy was concerned, and there were few individual complaints."

Nowadays, says Aslanian, this is no longer true. "Today the child's first passage from exclusively parental to dispersed responsibility takes a variety of forms. The next transition point, from school to work, is almost an emergency area, characterized by 15 to 50 percent unemployment rates for some groups in some regions of the country. Lifetime jobs are now rarities. As technology creates more and more specialized occupations and obliterates old crafts, people change careers three, four, or even more times. Women's combining a career with motherhood or a career with other roles creates a whole new set of transitions. At what used to be the final passage point—retirement—the sudden statutory scuttling of mandatory retirement at age 65 reflects political realization that the fastest-growing age group of voters and taxpayers is rethinking the sufficiency of security alone."

Recently, Aslanian conducted a survey of over 1,500 reentry adults in order to find out what had motivated their decision to return to school. Eighty-three percent answered that they wanted to learn to cope with changes in their lives. When questioned further as to what those changes were specifically, the following responses were given:

Changes in career: 56% (slightly lower for women only)
Major types of changes mentioned:
- Moving into a new job.
- Adapting to a changing job.
- Advancing in a career.

Changes in family situation: 16% (slightly higher for women only)
Major types of changes mentioned:
- Getting married.

- Becoming pregnant.
- Children moving through school.
- Getting divorced.
- Moving to a new location.
- Acquiring a new house or apartment.
- Increase in family income.
- Rising cost of living.
- Injury or illness of family member.
- Retirement of spouse.
- Death of family member.

Changes in approach to leisure: 13%

Changes in desire for artistic expression: 5%

Changes in health: 5%

Changes in level of spirituality: 4%

Changes in desire to be a better citizen: 1%

The Triggers of Change

The trigger for Abbie Rubenfeld's transition was her divorce three years ago. "Larry and I had a life plan," she says. "I was going to put him through law school, and, when he was working and established, he'd support me in finishing my counseling degree. Phase one worked beautifully. He became a lawyer and, within three years, achieved partnership in a large corporate law practice. When it came time to reciprocate, though, Larry had changed his mind."

By then, the couple had two children, and Abbie says she'd planned to attend school nights while her husband took care of the house and kids. "But suddenly he was never home," she says. "He began spending evenings and weekends at the office and was never there when it was time for me to leave for school. One day, he came home at 10:30 in the morning and told me he was moving out. He'd fallen in love with another lawyer, he said, and though he'd tried for a year to work it through, it hadn't happened."

Two weeks later, Abbie and her husband filed separation papers. "Initially," she says, "I trusted him to do what was right by me and our children. It took about three months before I realized that what he thought was right in terms of a financial settlement had nothing to do with my thinking on the subject."

Abbie started looking for a job, but, she says, "there wasn't much demand for an untrained woman with two small children. That's when I started thinking about going back to school. On a whim, I made an appointment with a career counselor at a local college. She showed me how I could finish my degree in two years attending the weekend program and—surprise of surprises—told me I was eligible for all kinds of financial aid."

Abbie Rubenfeld graduated last fall with a Bachelor of Arts in elementary education. She says that besides what she learned from her course work, she learned three lifetimes' worth of "stuff about myself. I found out, for example, that I didn't have to fold up when I was afraid of not being good enough. That I could make a plan for handling my fear and stick to it until I came out the other end." She also learned, she says, that she could take care of herself, something she doubted in the weeks after her husband left.

Abbie now teaches fifth grade at the same school attended by her children. "We leave together, come back together, and have the same vacations," she says. "But I still want to get my degree in counseling, so I'm thinking about going back to graduate school. My life has turned out to be a little different from the way I'd originally planned it, but—who knows—maybe I'm happier than I would have been in the old arrangement."

In Marisa Hernandez's case, the transition came when she realized that she deserved more out of life than an endless series of boring jobs. In 1972, she moved here from Honduras determined to make a better life for herself than the one she had had back home.

At the time, Marisa spoke not one word of English, but she took language classes at night and worked at low-paid, menial jobs by day. Eventually, she worked her way into a position as a bookkeeper. "I thought I'd died and gone to heaven," says Marisa of that time. Soon, however, she'd switched to an even better paid job typing index cards for a small import company. "For a while," she says, "I thought I was as happy as I could ever be." The change, when it came, came in an instant.

"One day, it was 5 o'clock and I still had hundreds of cards to do. My boss said he needed them that day and that I had to finish before I could go home. Suddenly I realized that I hadn't traveled all the way from another country to spend the rest of my life typing index cards. That week, I enrolled in the applied science program at the local university."

Recently, Marisa was forced to take a leave of absence from her studies because of an ongoing struggle with rheumatoid arthritis. "But I got back to school as soon as I could," she says. "There are many difficulties in being both a working woman and a student, and the only way to move beyond them is to be strong and push yourself to succeed, even on those days when you think it might be easier to fail. In my mind, that's the biggest difference between those who make it and those who don't." When Marisa receives her Associate in Applied Science degree in the fall, she will go into computer programming.

When Alexis Morgan's youngest child went off to school two years ago, she decided to do what she'd been putting off for half her life: finishing her college education. "For twenty-three years," she says, "I was very happy being a homemaker and the mother of four. Suddenly though, the house was empty, and, for the first time ever, I really took a look at my life. What I saw were large blocks of empty time and a marriage that was in serious trouble.

"One night," she says, "I went to bed, nothing particular on my mind. The next morning I woke up knowing as surely as I knew my name that I was going back to school. Two years later, I can't say I've gotten much support from either my husband or my children. My children I can understand. They just want me to be there the way I've always been. My husband, though, comes from a family that thinks education is wasted on women. He's constantly telling me that if I want to do something useful, I should get a job. But, the amazing thing is, I don't care. After twenty-four years, it's time I did something for me."

Alexis will graduate this year with a combined degree in English literature and history. After that, she says, she wants to go to graduate school to study "maybe personnel administration."

"Just recently I took a career placement test and was told I'd be good in some kind of administrative social service field. That's nice to know, but it's way in the future. More important is right now and the dozens of new things I'm learning about myself every single day. It took me forty-four years, but I finally learned, for example, that I don't need anybody's approval—not even my husband's—to feel good about myself."

Recruiting the Adult Woman: A Change in Strategy

While some school officials say that the sudden influx of adult women students has taken them completely by surprise, most point to preparation plans that are, in some cases, five to ten years old.

"If you were at all tuned in to the demographics of our society— and school administrators certainly should be—you would easily have foreseen that in the 1980s large numbers of women would turn to education as their ticket to a better life," says Donald MacIntyre, President of John F. Kennedy University in Orinda, California (a school that he characterizes as "the first private institution founded to serve midcareer adults"). "For one thing, women tend to interrupt their education three times as often as men do, usually for reasons having to do with family. For another, only half as many women as men are employed, and most of them are in menial jobs."

The bottom line, says MacIntyre, is that women are coming back to school because they *have* to. As the national trend continues away from a society based on manufacturing and toward one based on service industries and advanced technology, women know that their surest ticket of admission is education, whether they're entering the job market for the first time or upgrading their career. The chart on the next page shows the value of education in terms of dollars and cents.

"The huge numbers of people needing retraining have caused our school to almost double in size," says Steven Zwerling, Associate Dean of the New York University School of Continuing Education. Reentry women, according to Zwerling, contribute significantly to the fiscal solidity of NYU. "Therefore," he says, "we have devised a number of specific strategies geared not only to recruiting them but to keeping them once they've been admitted.

"For one thing, while many schools keep a student's name in their computers for only a year, we keep inquiries alive for five years. The reason? Our studies have shown that for adults, the decision to go back to school takes an average of three to seven years to come to fruition. Also, we've found that they typically wait until the last minute to enroll so that they can say, 'Oh well, I tried, but it's too late.' We enroll adult students into the second week of the semester, and we do it in one day so there's no opportunity for them to be paralyzed by fear and change their minds."

Zwerling's commitment to the adult learner is best typified, though, by his recent study on attrition rates. "We were horrified when we found that adults who begin college with no previous credits had a lower than one in ten chance of finishing. Furthermore, most of them—especially if they started in the fall—dropped out right after spring semester. What we suspected was that, after

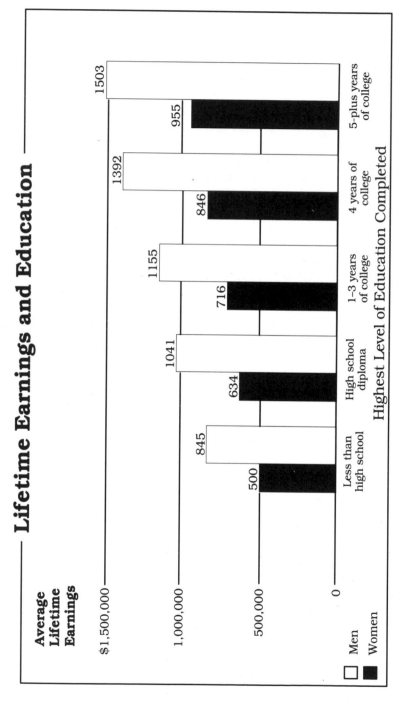

Lifetime Earnings and Education

Average Lifetime Earnings

$1,500,000

1,000,000

500,000

0

| | 1503 | 1392 | 1155 | 1041 | 845 |
| | 955 | 846 | 716 | 634 | 500 |

5-plus years of college · 4 years of college · 1–3 years of college · High school diploma · Less than high school

Highest Level of Education Completed

☐ Men
■ Women

Source: Lifetime Earnings for Men and Women in the U.S., Bureau of the Census.

a summer off, they enjoyed the free time so much that they didn't want to go back to doing papers and taking tests. We theorized that if we could get them to go to school in the summer, they'd stay in the program until they finished."

And so NYU implemented its "summer sale"—now institutionalized as part of its adult education strategy—whereby students were given as much as a quarter to a third off on tuition if they took at least one course in the summer. "What we found," says Zwerling, "is that more than half returned in the fall and kept on going."

At Smith College, where adult women make up 15 percent of the 2,600 students, returnees are recruited into a program created specifically for women whose education was previously interrupted—the Ada Comstock Scholars Program. The "Adas," as they are generally known, can take as long as they want to earn their degrees, and financial aid for those in need is virtually guaranteed.

The program, says its director, Eleanor Rothman, is only eight years old, but already it has expanded from 16 to 161 scholars. She hastens to point out that the level of achievement for this group is far higher than for traditional students. Twenty percent graduate Phi Beta Kappa, and 34 percent graduate with honors. "These are serious women," she says, "who may have taken a long time to come back, but once they're here, look out. I'd like to see us enroll many more."

Other colleges, like western Washington's publicly financed Fairhaven College in Bellingham, recruit students with the promise that they'll be able to design their own programs totally, work one-on-one with faculty members on independent studies, and study and participate in internships anywhere in the nation or, as is sometimes the case, abroad.

Marcy Austin is 32 and recently graduated with a B.A. in education, which is allowing her to make the switch from graphic arts to teaching. "The ability to go through a program I saw as relevant rather than one designed by someone who had never met me was what made me go back. I don't think I could have sat in a classroom doing stuff not consistently and specifically tied in to my needs."

At the University of California, Santa Cruz, a school with a large population of students with children, there's now an innovative parent locater program that allows children's schools to reach a parent anywhere on campus at almost a second's notice.

And at Pittsburgh's Chatham College, a small liberal arts school for women, adult students with children can live in Berry

Hall, a separate, renovated dorm that is convenient and affordable ($350 a month, including utilities, for mother and child) and has day-care facilities nearby.

To Don Bishko, Dean of the School of Business at the State University of New York College at New Paltz, colleges don't do nearly enough to attract reentry women. "They're the best students we have," he says. "They're the most organized, the most dedicated, and the most devoted. So we get into this way of thinking that says they'll take care of themselves. What happens is we wind up giving the bulk of our attention to the young kids, when what we should be doing is rolling out the welcome mat for these women."

Bishko, whose wife, Patricia, returned to school six years ago to study for a degree in psychological counseling, says that almost all the business school's valedictorians turn out to be single mothers who have returned to school. "Working mothers have a sense of efficiency and time management that other students never need to develop," he says. "They may only have 15 minutes to study, so they've learned to develop a style of concentration that enables them to get an hour's worth of work done in that time, and done well."

Reentry Women and Academic Achievement

In the years when they wrapped up their lives at 40, many people believed that three things happened as you got older: you got slower, your memory faded, and your intellectual powers decreased.

Janice Shauron, 51 years old and a recent graduate with a 3.8 average, remembers her preenrollment jitters. "I thought," she says, "that over the years my brain cells might have shriveled. I'd tell myself, 'You're smart, you can do it,' and then I'd see these young kids carrying 18 credits to my 3 and think, 'Oh God, please don't let me flunk out.'"

Today, we know that being over 30 has nothing to do with how well you think. In fact, a number of studies—most notably one done by Stanford University researchers comparing the intellectual ability of younger students with that of older returnees—showed absolutely no difference. Other research has measured the academic achievements of older female students against those of their younger counterparts and has shown the adult women scoring an average of 10 percentile points better on a scale of national grade distribution. They earned more A's, an equal number of B's and C's, and fewer D's and F's than the younger women. In another study, this one done at the University of Michigan, 91 percent of reentry women were earning grades equal to or better than the ones they had earned during their earlier attempts at higher education.

One reason older students do so well is that they are generally so thoroughly goal oriented. Meggie Sherman, who graduated with a 4.0 grade point average after being out of school fifteen years, remembers that she never got good grades in high school, using any excuse not to study. "Academic achievement didn't matter as much as my extracurricular activities," she says. "Now I know that there's a direct connection between what I'm learning and what I want to do in life."

Another woman who entered school at the age of 53 described herself as a "robot student" the first time she went to college. "I only did what I was told to do, and I did it with minimal input. Now," she says, "I love being in school. I'm motivated by the reading and writing because I know where it will get me."

"There *are*, however, things that separate the adults from the kids," says Ruth Dinerman, Assistant to the Director of Reentry Programs at New York University. "They're just not as measurable as intelligence quotas. They have more to do with the affective domain, the ways in which you *use* what's in the brain."

To Dinerman and others who deal with reentry women on a day-to-day basis, what differences there are fall into four major categories:

1. Life experience
2. Motivation
3. Academic behavior
4. Emotional problems

Life Experience

"I teach a course in reading skills for prospective teachers of elementary school students," says Sheila McAuliffe, Professor of Reading Instruction at Purdue University Calumet in Hammond, Indiana. "Many of the traditional undergraduates have little to no experience with small children. To them, teaching a child to read involves maybe reading to them a while, maybe teaching them a few words, and then — poof! — like magic, the kids are supposed to be able to read.

"My older students, on the other hand, have children of their own, and if not, they at least have years of exposure to other people's children. They've seen children fail, and they know enough to raise questions. I don't have to do much to get my message across to them."

Another professor, this one from the Department of Social Sciences at the University of Colorado, cites her own experience of returning to graduate school after fifteen years of working for a local real estate firm. "Those of us who were older had a wealth of life experience to bring to the classroom," she recalls. "Most of us had been involved in some kind of political or protest movement or some kind of human rights activity. We had seen and done a lot before we decided to go back to school, and we were very motivated, very organized, and very eager to shape the agenda for our learning.

"The young kids — and let me tell you, they *really* seemed young at the time — had all the energy in the world, but they had no sense of what life was about. Their questions were rather vague and narrow, and their arguments were based on such incredibly limited experience that, after a while, we all found ourselves groaning whenever one of them would get the floor."

Motivation

According to Barbara Kerr, Assistant Professor of Counselor Education at the University of Iowa College of Education, women almost always drop out of school for reasons having to do with others. "They cheerfully and compliantly give up their goals in order not to inconvenience other people," she says. "They trade academic dreams for the tugs of family, and, in many cases, come to rethink those trades after their children are grown."

For those who choose to return, the decision is treated as a precious second chance to fulfill a long-deferred dream. Most people in higher education who deal with reentry women on a day-to-day basis comment on this vision and on the effect it has in producing a particularly high level of motivation, especially compared to what is often referred to as the "limited-to-nonexistent" motivation of the younger student.

"Let's face it," says Mary Beth Iverson, Assistant Director of Admissions at the College of St. Catherine in St. Paul, Minnesota, "most traditional students are in school because their families expect them to be there. They never even considered any other options, all their friends are in school, and it's a fairly passive choice for them to fill out the admissions information.

"For returning students, however, the goal is usually fairly clear. They're in school because they want a better job, or they want to make changes in their life following a divorce. Whatever it is, they have direction. Where they're going is much clearer, and, as a result, their motivation for taking the steps to get there is much greater."

Many psychologists feel that motivation is the number one precursor to success, irrespective of ability. What they're saying is, in other words, if you want to, you will.

Academic Behavior

The biggest disadvantage facing the returning woman is that—at least at the beginning—she's an outsider. Younger students know the routine. They know how to get the courses they want, which professors to avoid, and which professors have what quirks. They know how to use the library and how to get a computer search done to cut their research time in half. They know how much time it takes to study for a lit exam and how to arrange their schedule so that they can have the time they need. In short, they're professional students.

Returners, on the other hand, have likely forgotten all of the above, if they ever knew it in the first place. And because they've been out of school for a while, they initially find themselves having problems with such things as concentration, writing papers, and getting the most important information from the text. Add to that the much-discussed statistics that show women in general to be lacking in math skills, and the picture becomes fairly bleak.

On the other hand (and somehow there's *always* another perspective), returning women have had many years' experience facing and overcoming problems in their life. They have a will to succeed that, in most cases, has enabled them to move from problem to solution in the shortest amount of time possible. In fact, many studies show that returning women take on the average only six weeks to boost their school skills to a point of functionality. Even in math.

Judith Coan, a New York–based psychotherapist and director of a counseling center, describes the problems faced by a returning woman in terms of "needing to crack the code."

"A woman who goes back to school after being part of the working world—and I insist on including homemakers—has a number of skills that need only a slight retooling for the world of academia. It's not a question of 'can I do it?' It's a question of 'how many steps does it take, and where do I go to learn what the steps are?' All we're lacking is the confidence that says, 'I'm capable.'

"In a way, our humility is one of our strengths. It causes us to reassess ourselves constantly and make changes where change is needed. In another way, it saps our energy, in that we're always doubting whether or not we can do it. We need to strike a more self-serving balance between the two."

Many schools offer courses specifically for returners in such areas as writing a research paper, time management, and math skills. Often, counseling centers offer skills assessment tests, so that the reentry student knows, before she gets into the classroom, whether she needs to spend some extra time sharpening her work in a particular area.

One area of academic behavior where returning women usually shine is in relationship to their instructors. For one thing, because returning students are older, professors seem more like their peers, like ordinary men and women who can be questioned and challenged. Also, returners are more used to questioning authority than younger students. They have more control over their lives and are used to making decisions about what works for them and what doesn't.

As one professor puts it, "Older students, especially women, are more inclined to question material that's presented. My reading lists, for example, usually have about twenty books listed. The kids know that if they read one all the way through and skim one or two more, they'll know enough to pass. The women, however, have usually sacrificed a lot to get here, and they're not happy with just getting by. They want to know which books are better than others, which ones will zero in on exactly their areas of concentration, which ones cost more than others. They want the class to work for them, and that includes me. It sounds like I'm saying they're a pain, but after so many years of having my word be unquestioned law, I have to say they give me new life."

Another professor points out that when he sees returners in the class, he knows that he had better do three things: cut out most of the jokes, start on time and end on time, and be prepared to stay after class for questions.

"These are people," he says, "who simply don't have time for the usual professorial flaunting of the ego. They let you know from the first minute that you're there to serve *them*."

Emotional Problems

Malcolm Knowles, author of a number of books on adult education, among them *The Adult Learner, A Neglected Species* (Knopf,

New York), says that the biggest problem faced by returners is their "astounding lack of self-esteem."

"There's a kind of negative self-image that's been developed from years out of academia," he says of reentry students, "and now, as they come back to school, they're almost always wondering, 'Will I look dumb? Will I look silly? Will I fail?'"

The fact is, he says, that the longer you've been out of school, the more time you've had to stew over how poorly you really write papers or how terrible you really are at simple calculations. The blocks established have been set in stone and require a concerted effort to budge. "That doesn't mean," says Knowles, "that it can't be done. Just that you have to acknowledge your sticking areas and reach out for help to get over them."

Most returning women also are saddled with the need to balance their education against a host of other responsibilities. Most work (70%), most have spouses (58%), most have children (51%–36% are single parents), and many have budgetary constraints. In addition, spouses and children are often resentful of the time spent on school-related work, creating stressful crises of loyalty.

According to Terry Lahti-Gadge, Director of Admissions for the College of St. Catherine in St. Paul, one of the chief problems faced by returning women is their great need for a support group composed of people going through the same experience. "It's ironic," she says, "that here you have all these women who could really help each other in terms of building confidence and self-esteem, and what happens is that, because of the obligations piled on them by the decision to go back to school, they don't have time to spend in the student lounge or over in the women's center talking to each other."

"At New York University we have a series of survival courses geared especially to our returning adults," says Ruth Dinerman. "I hire the instructors for these courses, and the most important thing I look for is a teacher who can develop a sense of 'group.' Adults, especially because they don't have the luxury of hanging around afterward, need to get as much support as they can from the class situation."

It's up to You

If you're considering going back to school, the first question to ask yourself is "Do I really want to do this?" Forget about how expensive it is or how you never did very well in school. The important thing is hearing yourself say this is what you want.

There's an ancient Chinese proverb from the province of Shanghai that says, "First decide you are going on the journey, then begin the figuring of how to get there."

Chapter

2

Now That You've Decided

Having decided to go back to school, right about now you're probably driving yourself crazy over one or more of the following:

- Will you be able to juggle your schedule so you have enough time for everything?
- How will your decision affect your relationships with family and friends?
- Do you have the necessary skills to make it, and, if not, what can you do to develop them?

Managing Your Time

Let's start with the element most tied to your future success and sanity: time management. Contrary to what you may believe, going to school does not mean you'll automatically have less time. What it does mean, however, is that you will need to use what time you have efficiently.

The first step is to get on intimate terms with your daily schedule. Compared to the problems *usually* faced when dealing with intimacy, this is a simple process best accomplished by making a list of everything you do for a week.

Make absolutely sure you leave nothing out. Draw up a series of boxes for each day of the week, and fill in your activities at the appropriate time. After a week, go over the chart and ask yourself the following questions:

1. Which things on this list are absolutely necessary?
2. Which things can I do without?
3. Which things that I consider very important am I not giving enough time to?

4. Which things that I don't consider important at all am I spending a great deal of time on?

Your answers should guide you in creating a schedule that both maximizes your time allotment for crucial activities and eliminates those that do nothing to serve your current needs. If you can force yourself to cut and slash away dead space in your schedule objectively, you'll probably find a niche just large enough for your new school-related time requirements.

When you do start school, buy yourself an appointment book small enough to carry with you at all times. Each week, fill in all the things that never vary: classes, work, exercise time, whatever is a constant in your life. Be realistic about how much time is required for each activity. Then plan slots for the things you consider to be essential, such as studying and spending time with your family. Avoid the impulse to consider this as "slotting the family into your schedule." The reality is that the more prepared you are in terms of knowing what you'll be doing and when, the less time you'll spend wondering whether you have time to stop in at your daughter's piano recital, for example. A quick look at your schedule, and you'll *know* whether you can spare the hour and a half.

Somewhere, maybe alongside your weekly schedule of activities, keep a running list of things that need doing *if* a slot opens up. That way, when a spare hour does materialize, you won't waste half of it wondering what to do.

Alan Lakein, in his book *How to Get Control of Your Time and Your Life* (New American Library, New York), suggests a program for learning the "skill" of effective time use:

- Keep a daily "to do" list.
- Consider that only two out of every ten items on that list are really worth doing.
- Concentrate your efforts on these high-priority items; don't get bogged down in insignificant tasks, no matter how quick and easy they are to do.
- Determine your most productive time of day, and reserve it for prime projects. Don't squander prime time on such routine tasks as reading the newspaper, answering the mail, or making the beds.
- Schedule routine tasks for non-prime-time hours when your energy level is at a low point.
- Try to do the same things at the same time every day. This conserves energy by cutting down on indecision. What you

are doing is generating energy through habit—the habit of planning meals, attending a class, going to a meeting, etc.

- Always reserve at least an hour of uncommitted time each day to accommodate crises and other unexpected events.
- Think of the time spent waiting for a bus, a doctor, or a professor as "found time," not lost time. Learn always to have something with you to do during these "found" moments.
- Don't waste time worrying about failures. Think of each mistake as a learning experience that will bring you closer to an eventual success. Studies have shown that people who hoped and strived for success were happier and accomplished more than those who feared and accepted failure.

If all this scheduling makes you yearn for just a little spontaneity, remember that your student days are numbered. At some point, they will be over, if only for a break between one degree and another. Also, while at first you might miss those opportunities to have lunch with friends whenever you want, chances are that after a while you won't even notice. Says a 34-year-old mother of two who combines her domestic role with that of a part-time bookkeeper and a student carrying 15 credits, "I've gotten to the point where I have to *plan* to buy soaking solution for my contact lenses or it just doesn't get done. But—and I can't believe I'm saying this—I've never been happier. My time is now so incredibly important that I continually strive to weed all the slack out of my schedule. What's left is what I've chosen to leave, and it feels good finally to have taken control of my life that way."

While it's great to talk about efficiency and maximizing one's schedule, however, equally important, and maybe even more so, is the ability to know your shut-off point, the point at which your body demands a break from the hectic pace of role-juggling. Says Dennis Jaffe, a California psychologist and stress-management consultant, "Too much efficiency is as ineffective as too little. The ideal is balance."

A 29-year-old returning student and full-time nurse puts it this way: "Once in a while I decide I've had it. All my circuits are on overload, and for me to push any further would be risking my health and sanity. What I do at that point is either cut class and sit under a tree with a bag of potato chips or, if it's more serious, call in sick and stay in bed all day with four or five trashy magazines. I rationalize the whole thing by telling myself how superproductive I'll be when I get back to the routine, and usually that's exactly what happens."

A Space of Your Own

Now that your schedule is pared down to only the most necessary activities (which, of course, are slotted in your appointment book in order of priority), it's time to turn to step two: the organization of what will be your work space.

No matter how small your space at home, you need a place to study and store your books, a place where you know you can leave that clipping about nutrition from yesterday's paper and nobody but nobody will touch it, a place that, by its very existence, establishes your identity as a "student."

Create a work area for yourself that has room in which to write, room in which to set up your books and reference materials for easy access, and—most importantly—room in which to keep your files. Files save vast amounts of time when used both as storage systems for notes and papers and as "idea collectors." Get in the habit of saving any scrap of information related to a particular area of interest and filing it for use as the backbone of a future term paper.

Also, try to organize your schedule so that you go to your work space every day. What you do there will vary; sometimes you'll study, whether that means memorizing notes for a test or reading another chapter of the text; sometimes you'll work on a paper or arrange the information you took down at yesterday's lecture; sometimes you'll simply sit there and daydream (see next paragraph). The important thing is to establish continuity, to keep what you're learning fresh in your mind. Learning, like exercising and playing the piano, is best accomplished when practiced every day.

When you think about daydreaming, you can probably still hear your mother's voice lecturing you on the uselessness of inactivity: "Don't just sit there, do something!" Contrary to those words of wisdom, however, daydreaming is not a waste of time. In fact, according to a number of psychological researchers, it is now considered to be a valuable part of the thinking process.

"We were wrong," says Jerome L. Singer, Professor of Psychology at Yale University. "Daydreams are not periods of inactivity. They are, instead, very vibrant examples of free-associational thinking that help us organize all the random information in our brains. When we daydream, we try out various solutions to problems and whittle the possibilities down to the one that makes the most sense. Our research has shown that daydreaming not only enriches life but leads to more creative thought and better physical and emotional health."

20

Learning to Delegate Responsibility

"When I first talked about enrolling as a full-time student," says Valerie Breyer, a 38-year-old mother of four, "my husband said don't worry, he'd 'help' with the kids and the housework. So we agreed on a schedule: he'd pick up the kids from the babysitter's and cook dinner, and I'd put them to bed and clean up.

"Well, what happened is that I'd come home exhausted around 6 o'clock, and he'd be sitting in front of the television eating ice cream with the kids. 'Where's dinner?' I'd ask, and he'd say, 'Oh, it'll be ready in a little while. Come sit down and relax.'

"I'd wind up doing the cooking *and* the cleaning, and when I would complain about it, he'd say I had to learn to let him do it on *his* schedule, not demand that he do it on mine."

Finally, says Valerie, she learned to put the time between walking in the front door and sitting down to dinner (about 45 minutes) to good use. "I now either go upstairs, fill the tub, and give myself a half-hour meditation and soak or change into my sweats and take a long walk around the neighborhood," she says. "By the time I sit down at the dinner table, I'm feeling relaxed and ready to be with my family."

According to a recent poll taken by the *New York Times,* women are still doing almost all the cooking and cleaning, despite the fact that three out of five work full-time. Of the almost 2,000 households surveyed, in 91 percent the woman did the cooking, the shopping, and most of the rest of the housework.

"One explanation for why women do more of the housework than men is that women feel bad if they don't do what's expected of them," says Ann Weber, a social psychologist and an associate professor at the University of North Carolina at Asheville. "And, in our society, women are — still — expected to take care of the home. When you look at it that way, you realize that it's not only the man who's to blame for the unequal division of household labor. Equally at fault are women who hang back from challenging certain assumptions for fear of losing the one identity they know they can count on: being a homemaker."

"Women are used to thinking of themselves as the primary caregivers," says Robin Sher, a San Francisco–based therapist. "In many cases, they're not open to somebody else's assuming even part of that responsibility. Many women say their husbands 'won't' do anything around the house or their children 'won't' pick up after themselves, when what's really going on is that these women aren't willing to let others take over what has always been their area of control.

"Let's face it, if you ask people to help you with *your* job, you're making it easy for them to say no because you've already identified the job as your responsibility. If you instead create the sense that this is their job, they'll know that if they want it done, they'll have to do it themselves or face its being left undone. The only problem, and this is usually where the system breaks down, is that women have to be willing to live with the possibility that the job may, in fact, be left undone. They have to let go of their total control over every aspect of the home."

As a student faced with too much work and too little time, you will have to learn to delegate many house-related chores formerly seen by family members as purely yours. The following questions should help you clarify the important issues in effecting such a change:

- Have I discussed with family members my feeling that chores should be shared by everybody?
- Have I made it clear that I am not asking them to "help" me in what is intrinsically "my job," but that everybody who lives in the house should share in its care?
- Am I open to having certain jobs done in a way that suits the style of the learner, or do I usually insist that my way is the only way?
- Have I let members of my family make their own mistakes while learning to do a certain job, thereby communicating that their learning is more important to me than the completion of the job?
- Am I willing to let the household fall into disarray while members adjust to the idea that I will no longer be sole caretaker?
- Am I willing to let go of my controlling homemaker role to the point where I can accept that how the house gets run might not be determined solely by me?
- Have I made it clear that I am no longer willing to assume total responsibility for running the household; that the discussion is not about *whether* chores can be shared but about how this will happen?

Before getting involved in any discussion about delegating house-related responsibilities, however, you should know what it is you want to delegate. Start by taking stock of the amount of time you spend cooking, shopping, cleaning, etc. Make a one-week chart similar to the one you made earlier. Fill in the house-related jobs you did each day, followed by how much time it took to do them. At the end of a week, ask yourself the following questions:

1. Which activities can be done less often?
2. Which activities can be done by somebody else?
3. Which activities can be done by me (or somebody else) in a more efficient manner?
4. Which activities can be eliminated?

"The key to making changes in your life is to start with a plan," says Mark Valenti, a New York–based therapist and time-management consultant for a number of Fortune 500 corporations. "No matter what the area of focus, the basic prescription is always the same. First, write down what you're doing in the present. Don't assume you know what it is because you've been doing it for twenty years. Then, look at the list and make some decisions about what needs to change. Prioritize them according to what changes can be made immediately, what can wait till next week, etc." Finally, says Valenti, *take action!*

Easing Your Children Through the Change

"She's never here, and when she is, she usually has her head stuck in a book. I used to bring my friends over after school and she'd always have snacks for us. Now I have to go over Timmy's house and wait for her to pick me up. Sometimes she's even late." These are the words of the 7-year-old son of a part-time reentry student at Maricopa Community College in Phoenix, Arizona.

The 15-year-old daughter of a full-time undergraduate student at Hood College in Frederick, Maryland, says, "I'm very proud of my mom for making the decision to go back to school. After Dad left, she spent a few years moping around the house, talking about how we couldn't make it on the money he sent. Sometimes she'd say she was afraid of the future, of maybe spending the rest of her life working as a waitress at the diner. I'd always tell her she could do anything she wanted. Now she's going to be a nurse in two years. We don't get to spend as much time together as we used to, but I can see she's really happy, so I guess in a way I'm happy too."

According to a recent survey, one out of every two reentry women has a child or children at home under the age of 18. Most worry, at least initially, about whether their new role as a student will be accepted by their families; whether the amount of time put into school-related work will harm their children; whether it is right even to want to do something so clearly for their own personal betterment.

The first step in dealing with these worries is to take a step back and look at the situation objectively. It is true that you will be bringing change to your home situation by going back to school and that children almost always respond poorly to change, at least initially. What is also true, however, is that in most cases, children adjust to change more quickly than adults. Which ones do and which ones don't is usually determined by how the situation is handled. The following paragraphs contain some tips designed to help ease your children into acceptance of your new school-related life.

Involve your children in the decision-making process from the minute you first start suspecting you will be going back to school. Don't, however, do it in a way that gives them power over the final yes or no. Simply explain your reasons for wanting to go back, even if those reasons have to do with fears about your financial future. Children may not talk about their observations, but that doesn't mean they haven't sized up what's going on. Chances are they already know why you want to go back, whether it's to get a better job or to give your life greater meaning. Your putting it on the table for discussion will enable them to deal with it and eventually accept it.

Find out what they would like from you in terms of time. Ask them whether it's important for you to be at sports events, for example, or at home every night for dinner. In most cases, you will be able to schedule your course load with those considerations in mind. If you can't, remember that children, like the rest of us, can handle not getting their way all the time if somebody cares enough to explain why not.

Involve your children in your school life. Talk to them about what you're learning, whom you're meeting, why you're so excited (or frustrated or disappointed). Be alert to the effects of your reporting. If you're a straight A student and your daughter is having trouble maintaining a B average, she might see you as competition. Take your children to the campus and show them where you take classes. Most schools offer movies, sporting events, concerts, and plays that the family can share.

Set up a system so that you (or somebody who can act for you) are reachable at all times. Post your schedule of classes on the refrigerator door, along with the relevant phone numbers. Make a list of backup people—friends and relatives—so that your child knows somebody will always be available.

Make time to spend with your child, even if you are pushed into a corner by end-of-term demands. Much of the resentment children feel over Mommy going back to school comes from sensing they've been replaced as number one in her heart. Often, especially when you're working under deadline pressure, that will be the case. Do your best to avoid winding up in that position, but if you do, be aware of the fine line between teaching your children that they're not always the center of the universe and understanding that sometimes they need you more than your studies do.

The Man in Your Life

In addition to worrying about the effect of going back to school on their children, many women also fear the reactions of the man in their life.

"Sam and I decided to live together instead of getting married because we thought we didn't need traditional definitions for how we felt about each other. We saw ourselves as stretching the limits of how committed relationships could be. In our minds, we were going to forge a fresh concept of partnership based on total trust and complete equality.

"Last year, I decided to go back to school to get a degree in teaching. After twelve years as a broker, I'd had it with the stress level and was willing to give up the money if it meant doing something I really loved. Well, when Sam heard about it, he hit the roof. He went from anger that he'd have to assume more of the house-related chores to disbelief that I could 'betray our life-style' by opting for such a cut in pay to worry over whether our relationship could survive such a change in direction."

The traditional role for a woman in our society is basically a nonassertive one. A woman who adheres to the model is both nonaggressive and largely dependent on others for her survival. Her mode of operation is to reach for consensus rather than provoke confrontation. She does not act like a leader, does not defend her own beliefs if they conflict with someone else's, and has a hard time making decisions. From very early on, she is taught to shape her life around the following tenets:

- Whether or not she works, her greatest fulfillment will come from marriage, home, and children.
- Her role is to live through and for others rather than for herself.

- She must look to men for both sustenance and status.
- She is at her best when emphasizing nurturing and life-preserving activities.

According to these principles, a woman who goes back to school rejects all or part of the traditional model of womanhood. For one thing, she has made a decision, a decision that is first and foremost designed for her own benefit. For another, when she's done, she will have boosted her earning potential so that she can, if she likes, be self-sufficient.

Many men are threatened by the assertiveness implicit in that kind of advancement. It's understandable when you look at the tape by which they've been programmed. They've been told ever since they were in diapers that their role in life was to be a "man," which, when translated, meant being strong and taking care of the woman in their life.

Now these same men see women moving to free themselves from the traditional limitations, and they're afraid. They fear women's becoming independent because they think the women will outgrow them or won't need them anymore. They fear women's taking over a role that they consider theirs by birthright, and they resent having to change their perception of themselves just because women changed theirs.

Many women who initially received tremendous support from the man in their life say that, as they got close to finishing their studies, the support dried up. "At first my husband was like my own personal cheerleader," says a 45-year-old computer programmer who recently graduated from Ohio State University. "When I'd talk about flunking out, he'd tell me how smart I was and even help me study for exams. But then, as I got closer to getting the degree and started talking about getting a job, he began to see that I'd probably be making more money than he and that he'd have to chip in with the housework. All of a sudden, he started making fun of me, telling me nobody would hire a woman with gray hair."

Each man shows his fears differently. For some, it takes the form of open disapproval that comes out in arguments, ultimatums, or mockery; for others, it shows up as silence: "Do whatever you want. Just don't talk to me about it."

Often, a man will speak with great enthusiasm about the return to school: "I'm glad Liz decided to go back. She's been complaining for years about her job, about how her boss never listens to her because she doesn't have a degree. Now she's studying to be a social worker, and I can see that she's much happier. The kids and

I have made sacrifices so that she could do this, but we all think it will be worth it in the end."

This same man's wife, however, tells a different story: "I've always worked, so Bob is used to having to do a few things around the house, like laundry and vacuuming. Now that I'm going to school three nights a week, though, I expected he'd do a little more. Ater all, the money I'm going to be making when I'm done will benefit both of us. But I walk in the door at 7:30 after being out all day, and he's sitting on the couch waiting for me to make dinner."

Mixed messages tell a lot about what's going on in a person's head. In some cases, the problem may be one of just not realizing the discrepancy, in which case the best thing to do is to talk the whole thing through. Be careful, however, to avoid accusations. "If you really cared about me, you would have seen how exhausted I was and started dinner yourself," does not come under the category of constructive talking.

Stick to descriptions of what's going on with you: "When I come home and dinner's not ready, I feel overwhelmed by all I have to do." Also, don't automatically assume that he's aware of everything you're feeling and is deliberately refusing to help out. *You* are the one who changed the situation; he may just be waiting for you to provide some clues as to how to proceed next.

Here are some final quick tips to help you figure out what those clues should be:

1. Organize your time so that you do things in slots. If you tell him you'll be done at 10:30, and you're still there at 1, expect resentment. Stick to your schedule.

2. Going back to school will increase your level of anxiety. Expect it. Do something every day to lower it, whether it's walking, bicycling, gardening, or whatever. No matter how tight your schedule, an hour spent getting yourself together will both boost your productivity and make you a much pleasanter person to be with.

3. Have fun with your mate. Even though you'd rather spend the time polishing that term paper, force yourself to do something the two of you enjoy. It will prevent you from a burnout down the road because you've spent too much time on your work, and it will create a bond between the two of you that will make it easier for him to support what you're doing.

Making the Grade

You've been out of school for a number of years. When you think about going back, the following fears rise to the surface:

- You won't be able to concentrate long enough to do all the reading that's required.
- You won't know how to write a paper.
- You were always terrible in math, and now you've forgotten the little you knew in the first place.
- You're not sure you ever knew how to use the library; you certainly know you don't know now.

Once again, relax. Take a step back, and look at the whole thing objectively. Heed the wisdom of the ancient proverb: "Everything we need to know we already know; it's just a question of remembering it."

When you're dealing with study skills, "remembering" is often just a matter of taking the steps necessary to bring that particular information back to the surface. For example, if you think you have problems with concentration or you think you read too slowly, you might want to buy a speed-reading workbook and put yourself through the suggested course even before enrolling in school. Two that are good are *Triple Your Reading Speed* by Wade E. Cutler (Arco, New York) and *Personalizing Reading Efficiency* by Lyle Miller (Burgess, Minneapolis). Both rely on the same principles:

- Training your eyes to take in a greater area of print.
- Setting a purpose before you begin to read.
- Learning to skim and scan material for important words and phrases.
- Keeping your eyes moving ahead despite the urge to look back to recheck information.
- Focusing your concentration through exercises performed before and after reading.

Each course takes from four to six weeks, and most people report significant increases in both speed and comprehension upon completion of the program.

Since most people who say they have problems with concentration usually also admit to having too many things on their mind, a good way to improve your ability to focus is by using a relaxation exercise that temporarily clears the mind.

"A relaxation skill is the most crucial element to improving learning ability," says Don Schuster, Professor of Psychology at

Iowa State University. "Anxiety interferes with learning. Any kind of anxiety, not just the type associated with the learning process itself. If you can rid an individual of anxiety, he or she is more likely to learn."

The following quick relaxation technique is a good one to use when you need to really focus your concentration:

- Close your eyes and take a few deep breaths. Starting with your toes and working through to your face, clench each body part as tightly as you can for a few seconds and then release, each time noticing the difference between the condition of tension and the condition of relaxation. Do your face, neck, shoulders, arms, chest, stomach, pelvis, legs, feet, and toes. Remember to keep breathing deeply throughout.
- When you've gone through the whole body this way, sit for a few minutes noticing your breath flowing in and out and the relaxed state of your body. Tell yourself how relaxed and wonderful you're feeling.
- Open your eyes, and get to work!

This kind of relaxation exercise takes no longer than 10 minutes. Yet most people who use it say that their ability to concentrate is instantly enhanced.

There are also a number of specific techniques that will help you in writing a research paper, and, fortunately, they too are learnable. For one thing, always make an outline; it lets you see the relationship between ideas and, in the long run, saves time and the need for multiple drafts. Also, make sure you collect enough information before you even start the paper. Nothing uses up time like sitting at your desk trying to create a ten-page paper from material that, at best, fills up two pages. Helpful books are *How to Write Themes and Research Papers* by Barbara L. Ellis (Barron's, New York), *The Random House Guide to Research Writing* by Thomas S. Kane and Peter J. Leonard (Random House, New York), and *Perfect Term Papers Step by Step* by Donald J. Mulkerne Jr. (Doubleday, New York).

In addition, you should have on hand a number of good reference books to help you with such things as definitions (*Webster's Riverside Dictionary*, for example), synonyms (*Roget's Thesaurus* is the standard work), and form (*Turabian's Guide for Writing College Papers* by Kate Turabian, University of Chicago Press).

You might also want to consider investing in an inexpensive computer that has a word processing program. While electronic typewriters and word processors let you type and edit papers, depending on the software you choose, a computer will help you do anything from creating spreadsheets to setting up poetry.

For roughly $500, you can buy a stationary computer (portable laptops are in the $1,000–$2,000 range). For $200, you can get a simple word processing program that has everything you need for writing papers. For an extra $150–$300, you can throw in a letter-quality printer. Forever after, this package will save you mountains of time editing and doing rewrites. Many computer stores run one- and two-day courses that teach you how to use both your computer and any software you've purchased. Continuing education departments of local community colleges also run short, inexpensive workshops in learning to operate computers.

If you need help with creative writing or if you find that your research papers get bogged down under constant rewriting, you might benefit from a simple little book called *Writing Down the Bones* (Shambhala Press, Boston). Its author, Natalie Goldberg, promotes a method called "freewriting" that involves putting your pen on the paper and not lifting it off for a period of 10 to 15 minutes, even if the only thing you write is "I have nothing to write."

"The aim," says Goldberg, "is to burn through to first thoughts, to the place where energy is unobstructed by social politeness or the internal censor, to the place where your mind actually sees and feels directly instead of turning out what it *thinks* it should think, see, or feel."

Goldberg suggests the following as the "bare-bones" 10- to 15-minute freewriting exercise:

1. Keep your hand moving. Don't pause to read the line you've just written. When you do that, you're stalling and trying to get control of what you're saying.
2. Don't cross out. That is editing as you write. Even if you write something you didn't mean to write, leave it.
3. Don't worry about spelling, punctuation, grammar. Don't even care about staying within the margins and lines on a page.
4. Lose control.
5. Don't think. Don't get logical.
6. Go for the jugular. If something comes up in your writing that is scary or naked, dive right into it. It probably has lots of energy.

Goldberg suggests her method not only for creative writing but for writing first drafts of research papers. "It sounds like it would take longer to first write out a whole unedited draft and then go back to put it in proper form," she says, "but your first writings are what give your papers life. Once you have the energy and the tone down pat, all you have to do is fill in the proper information."

If your particular sticking area is math, you will probably want to talk to your adviser about basic skills testing. Depending on the results, you might be better off taking a semester or two of remedial math (in many colleges, such courses can be taken for degree credit) rather than suffering the anxiety of sitting in a college algebra class not having any idea of what's going on. Some books you might consult on the subject are *All the Math You'll Ever Need—A Self-Teaching Guide* by Steve Slavin (Wiley, New York), *College Mathematics* (Barnes & Noble, New York), and *Mathematics Encyclopedia* by Max S. Shapiro (Doubleday, New York).

When it comes to library and research skills, the best thing is to schedule a meeting with the school librarian for a hand-holding tour of how your library works. Most school libraries have now installed some kind of computerized research facility. Some, like the library of the State University of New York College at New Paltz, have individual computer terminals where users can scan thousands of professional journals and periodicals for information about their particular topics. Others, like the Smith College library, have computerized card catalogs instead of wooden drawers full of cards for finding the names and locations of books dealing with specific topics.

Just about every school now makes use of computerized databases for research into a particular subject. To use such resources, you make an appointment with a research consultant in the library, fill out a form detailing what kind of information you need, and, within days, pick up a printout of whatever articles exist on your subject. Such searches cost anywhere from a few dollars to hundreds of dollars, depending on the number of articles available.

Finally, a word about the relationship between your body and your brain. "One of the absolute basics of good memory is a good diet," says Jane Bancroft, a University of Toronto professor who was one of the first to study the effect of poor health on memory and concentration. "If you don't eat properly, you don't nourish the brain. Food that is processed and loaded with additives, sugar, caffeine, too many fats, all contribute to a decrease in mental power."

"Taking care of your health is the number one way to achieve academic success," says Claude Fell Merzbacher of the Department of Natural Science at San Diego State University. Merzbacher recently gathered a group of thirty-one adult volunteers to test the effect of diet and exercise on mental functioning. For twenty-six days, each volunteer ate a high-fiber diet and exercised daily. Follow-up tests showed that the group scored higher on such things as verbal fluency, quick clear thinking, intellectual efficiency, and perceptiveness.

In another study, adults in their forties took part in a ten-week walking and jogging program. A similar group remained sedentary. Then the researchers tested both groups' reaction time, one of the things scientists use to measure how well we recall things. The exercisers beat the group of sedentary people hands down.

"None of us were surprised by the results," says Ronald Lawrence, one of the researchers connected with the study. "Exercise and a good diet lead to better health, and the simple fact is that people in better health perform better whatever they have to do."

You may think that, with your new school-related responsibilities, you have no time for a health-promotion program. If so, read the words of one recent graduate from the University of San Francisco's business program: "When I first entered the program, I regularly ate junk food from the cafeteria instead of taking time to prepare wholesome meals. I also cut regular exercise from my schedule, figuring that, as a full-time student and part-time secretary, something had to go. Well, within a year I'd had four colds that each lasted for weeks, and I was progressively having a harder and harder time concentrating, in spite of the fact that I loved my schoolwork.

"Now I eat better and run regularly, and I haven't been sick in two years. Sometimes when I start my evening run, my head is in a fragmented state, full of worry about papers I have to write, tests I have to take. When I finish, I'm clear about how and when everything will get done. My mind and body are one, and my schoolwork gets done in half the time."

Chapter

3

What Kind of School? The Traditional Options

What kind of school you choose depends on what you want from your educational experience. If, for example, you want to take a few introductory courses to find out whether or not you're student material, your best bet might be a two-year college, which is both easier to get into than a four-year one and much less expensive. On the other hand, if you want to get the college degree you've been dreaming of for fifteen years, the four-year college or university is probably going to meet more of your needs, although you can always start at a two-year college and then transfer.

In this chapter, you'll find a list of questions to ask about any school you might be considering, as well as information about the various types of *traditional* educational experiences, the ones where you take regularly scheduled instruction from a teacher in a classroom. Included are:

- Two-year colleges (interchangeably referred to as junior colleges or community colleges).
- Four-year colleges and universities.
- Graduate schools.
- Trade and vocational schools.

Things to Investigate Before Choosing a School

Licensing

A vocational or trade school should be licensed by your state's postsecondary school licensing bureau. If the school's brochure doesn't indicate this, check with the department of education in your state.

Accreditation

Accreditation applies only to degree-granting institutions and means that the school has passed a thorough examination of its educational quality, teaching ability, and administrative integrity. Accreditation is awarded by an accrediting agency recognized by the U.S. Department of Education and is usually listed in the first few pages of a school's catalog. It is always better to attend a school that is accredited, both in terms of being able to transfer your credits elsewhere and in terms of applying to graduate school later, should you decide to.

Courses

If you can, talk to some graduates of the school you're considering. Ask if they think the courses they took were generally up-to-date, well-rounded, and of high quality. Ask if their studies adequately prepared them for an employment field. Were the courses taught by the instructors whose names were listed in the catalog or by graduate students assigned by the instructor? How often was each course offered?

Facilities and Equipment

How do the school's equipment and facilities compare with what's currently being used in the field? If the education is geared toward specific job training, does the school have a setup that duplicates the actual work environment? If you're enrolled in a film program, for example, does the school have enough video cameras to go around, or will the courses be mostly theoretical? Most answers can be had from the department head, who, believe it or not, usually can be talked into showing you around.

Placement Assistance

Does the school help find jobs for graduates? Does the school have linkups with the job community? Is there some kind of job counseling service that provides students with the resources to find their own jobs?

Two-Year Schools

Of the more than 12 million people currently pursuing an education beyond high school, almost half are enrolled in two-year colleges. Sixty-five percent of these are part-time students, and approximately 40 percent eventually transfer to a four-year school. A few of the reasons why two-year colleges have become so popular with adults are detailed in the following paragraphs.

Two-year colleges are much more receptive than four-year schools to students who only want to take one or two courses a semester rather than a complete course load. Many also allow students to take as long as they want to get their degree, as opposed to four-year schools, where there is a definite time limit.

Admission to two-year colleges is easier than admission to four-year schools for those whose academic background has been less than superior. In fact, most two-year colleges offer a host of remedial services for students needing help with reading or math or even language proficiency. Also, most have open admissions policies by which anybody with a high school diploma or its equivalent is automatically admitted. Others may have minimum requirements, but these usually involve nothing more stringent than the submission of high school records or letters of recommendation.

Two-year schools offer large numbers of courses designed specifically for adults, who are often afraid of "not being good enough." Titles range from Assertiveness Training to Coping with Transition. Also, there are usually dozens of orientation courses to guide students through the first few months after enrollment— things like Honing Your Study Skills and Learning to Do Computer Research. In many cases, such courses can even be taken for credit.

Expenses at a two-year college are minimal compared to those at a four-year college. At many public two-year colleges, the tuition for residents of the particular community or state can be less than $75 per credit. The only other expenses are usually the cost of books and student fees, which are almost always less than $25. Private two-year colleges charge more, although not nearly as much as the private four-year schools.

Two-year colleges offer classes at times that are more convenient for working people. Since the overwhelming majority of students in a two-year college hold full-time jobs, classes are arranged to fit *their* schedule. Some even offer weekend courses through which students can complete their entire degree program.

There is probably a two-year college nearby. Many community colleges have extension programs that are located in high schools or in office buildings. Adelphi University's Commuter Program offers courses that are taught on the Long Island Rail Road so that commuters, who often travel 2 hours one way, can earn college credit while traveling to work.

Because the majority of two-year colleges are located within the community, they are more likely to have established links with the local job sector. In many cases, they can provide you with the names of companies who will hire you immediately after graduation.

Two-year colleges are much more career oriented than their four-year counterparts. A wide variety of degree and certificate programs are offered to prepare students for immediate employment. Two-year programs require approximately 65 semester hours of course work (about twenty-two courses) and usually lead to one of three degrees (not all of which are available at every school):

- Associate in Arts (A.A.)
- Associate in Science (A.S.)
- Associate in Applied Science (A.A.S.)

The fields of study offered in each degree program usually depend on the availability of certain types of job in the locality. Currently the areas most in demand, especially by women, have to do with either communications, information services, or the health sciences. A sample offering of fields of study leading to specific associate degrees might include the following:

Associate in Arts

Acting	Landscape architecture
Art	Political science
Communications	Psychology
Dance	Public administration
Economics	Sociology
Foreign languages	Theater

Associate in Science

Accounting	Information processing
Banking	Nursing
Business administration	Physical education
Computer science	Prechiropractic
Criminal justice	Pre–medical technology
Engineering science	Pre–physical therapy
Health education	Security administration

Associate in Applied Science

Accounting
Data processing
Fashion buying and
    merchandising
Food service
    administration
Hotel technology
    administration
Medical laboratory
    technology
Paralegal
Physical therapist's assistant
Radiological technology
Respiratory care
Secretarial science
Surgical technology

A sample of certificate programs (also referred to as professional diploma programs) offered at two-year schools includes the following:

Certificate Programs

Geriatric health-care
    specialist
Information systems auditing
Insurance
Photography
Real estate
Small-business
    management
Systems analysis
Word processing

For those who aren't sure what direction they want to take, two-year colleges are usually well equipped to serve as guides to information resources available in the community. They almost always offer free of charge both aptitude testing and career testing and placement. Also, they usually have various kinds of counseling services, including counseling for drug and alcohol abusers.

There are, however, a number of disadvantages in attending a two-year school. Many courses will not be transferable if a student subsequently chooses to switch to a four-year college. Students should keep in close contact with an adviser, who will be able to recommend which courses generally will be accepted and which will not. A student who knows beforehand that she will be transferring at the end of two years should have her courses approved in advance.

Courses in popular subject areas fill up quickly, and a two-year college usually is not equipped to offer as many sections of a course as a larger four-year school is. Also, the course offerings in the more traditional academic areas, such as the liberal arts and the social sciences, may be very limited. A student may find herself with one or two semesters to go and not enough courses left to take in her field.

While most employers say they lean toward hiring workers who have some kind of degree, many jobs can be had without one. Prospective students should find out before enrolling whether a degree is really necessary. They should talk to employers and employees in the field they are thinking of entering. For example, a degree in word processing may not be necessary; on-the-job training may be just as valuable.

A good source of information on two-year colleges, including a state-by-state breakdown that lists tuition costs, programs offered, and financial aid possibilities, is *Peterson's Guide to Two-Year Colleges* (Peterson's, Princeton, New Jersey).

Four-Year Schools

These can be divided into three basic types:

- Universities
- Colleges
- Special interest schools

Universities

The terms "college" and "university" are often used to mean one and the same thing. They are not the same. A university is a collection of several colleges, each usually having its own dean, its own admissions requirements, and its own budget. As people who change majors find out, what happens at one such college may have absolutely nothing to do with what takes place at another.

A university offers graduate degrees as well as undergraduate degrees. Some offer master's degrees (for example, M.A. or M.S.); some also offer doctoral degrees (Ph.D., Ed.D., Psy.D., and professional degrees in law and medicine, among others). Opinions vary, however, on the value of staying on at one university for both undergraduate and graduate work. For the most part, it is considered wiser to study for each degree at a different school so that you have exposure to as many points of view as possible.

Because universities are large institutions, they usually have more in the way of services than colleges. Most university libraries, for example, now have individual computer stations for students doing research and on-site research consultants who can discuss your assignment needs and, for a fee, institute a computer search for all available information on your topic.

Universities are also more likely to have faculty members who are widely known as experts in their field and to offer a wider variety of courses that are available on a continuing basis. A university probably will have more in the way of counseling and career placement services than a small college, and it most likely will be in a better position to offer financial assistance to greater numbers of students.

Colleges

Unlike a university, a college is not divided into distinct schools. Therefore, it offers only a general or liberal arts education rather than the university's more diversified offerings, which can include professional and technical training.

While it is true that universities have the ability to offer more of everything, more may not always be better. For one thing, a larger school means a greater number of people using each facility. This can translate into a two-week wait for an appointment to meet with a research consultant or a registration process that takes days. For another, it means that school personnel are required to serve larger numbers of people, which can make them impersonal at the very time when a sympathetic ear is needed most.

Also, the smaller the school, the greater a student's interaction with faculty and staff. At a small college, students will probably know their professors personally, and their work most likely will receive a more individualized assessment. They probably will be on a first-name basis with any counselors and academic advisers they go to for direction. And finally, class size will be smaller, so they will have a better opportunity to get to know other students.

Special Interest Schools

In addition to the more than 1,500 general studies colleges in the United States, there are also a number of special interest schools that cater to specific groups or specific areas of job training. For the purposes of this book, we'll take a look at three of them: liberal arts colleges, specialized colleges, and women's colleges.

Liberal Arts Colleges

Following a ten-year decline in popularity, liberal arts programs are now experiencing a burst of renewed interest. One reason is the number of recent studies showing liberal arts graduates outperforming graduates of more specialized programs in a wide variety of job situations. Proponents say that while specialty studies teach students how to do a particular job, liberal studies teach students to think, a skill that transfers to any occupational situation.

Liberal arts colleges offer bachelor's degree programs for students whose interests are too wide-ranging to be satisfied by a single area of concentration. Liberal arts programs include courses in the humanities, the social sciences, the physical sciences, and the behavioral sciences, among others. The aim is not to master any one area of study but to create a well-developed sense of self and a solid understanding of the relationship between self and environment.

Specialized Colleges

These are schools that offer bachelor's degree programs in specific areas of concentration. If a student wants to become a businesswoman or an engineer or a musician, for example, she may want to consider a school focusing exclusively on that particular area. Her core courses (a quarter to a half of the total program) will be the same as those in other colleges, but the remaining two thirds will be focused on her specialty area.

Women's Colleges

A number of recent studies have focused attention on the wide range of differences, both biological and environmental, between men and women with respect to the learning process. For example:

- Only 52 percent of female high school seniors take trigonometry, as compared to 59 percent of the males. Comparable figures for calculus are 21 percent male, 15 percent female. In science, 51 percent of the males but only 35 percent of the females take physics, and 87 percent of the males but only 77 percent of the females take chemistry.
- The overwhelming majority of high school science and math teachers are men.
- The overwhelming majority of first-, second-, and third-graders have mothers who think their sons will do better in math than their daughters.
- In the nation's elementary schools, remedial reading classes (a boy's area of deficiency) outnumber remedial math classes (a girl's area of deficiency) two to one.
- On the basis of a number of recent studies, the Association of American Colleges concluded that while professors in colleges and graduate schools show male students how to use equipment and perform lab experiments, they do the work *for* female students. In general, male students receive more eye contact and far more of the professor's attention than do female students. "The classroom climate obviously affects women's learning and intellectual self-esteem," says the association's report. "Women students are much less likely

than their male counterparts to feel confident about their preparation for and their ability to do graduate work."

Proponents of women's colleges say that such findings illustrate the problems of trying to educate women in a system set up for and by men. The solution, they say, is to pull men out of the environment, both physically and in terms of their influence over the curriculum. Says Joyce Findron, a junior at Alverno College in Milwaukee, "I like the fact that Alverno is a women's college. The advantages of not having guys around outweigh the disadvantages. It's more relaxed. You can concentrate on your studies. You can control your social life. You don't have to be constantly worrying about how you look. When I graduate, I know that I'm going to be very happy I attended a women's college. It has enabled me to learn more."

While there are currently only 94 women's colleges in this country (down from 228 twenty years ago), a number of recent studies have shown a far greater rate of success for graduates of single-sex schools. For example, although women's colleges account for only 5 percent of female college graduates, one third of the board members of the nation's top 1,000 companies are graduates of women's colleges . Of the twenty-seven female members of Congress as of August 1989, 44 percent received their degree from a women's college.

Researchers at the University of Michigan recently conducted a study of 1,250 girls in both single-sex and coed secondary schools. Results showed that girls from the single-sex schools were more likely to enjoy math; do more homework; have higher test scores in vocabulary, reading, math, and science; and show more ambition in terms of a career. A follow-up study of the same students in college showed that the gains continued. Graduates of single-sex secondary schools went to more selective colleges, were more interested in politics, reported being more satisfied with their college experiences, and were more apt to apply to graduate schools and choose nontraditional careers. In fact, according to a 1985 study done by the Women's College Coalition, students at women's colleges tended to major in biology, physics, and math— all traditionally male-dominated fields—40 percent more often than their coeducational counterparts.

Women's colleges are generally small, and, as you might expect, generally more geared toward the special concerns of women students, such as day care and family housing. For further information on women's colleges, contact the Women's College Coalition, Suite 1001, 1101 17th Street, NW, Washington, DC 20036 (202-466-5430).

Graduate Schools

While reentry students, until recently, were somewhat of an oddity on the undergraduate college campus, they have always been the norm in master's and doctoral degree programs. This is because a typical graduate student spends at least a few years working before deciding to go back to school.

If you're thinking about enrolling in a graduate program, chances are your reasons are very similar to the reasons of those who have chosen to go back for undergraduate study: you've gone about as far as you can in your job with the skills you have; you want to change careers and are opting for one of the more vocationally oriented graduate programs; or you are excited about a certain field and want to explore it on a higher level.

Regardless of why you are going back, you should consider the following facts about graduate study:

- Of the almost 2,000 accredited four-year schools in this country, less than half offer graduate programs. Chances are that, unless you live in a large metropolitan area, you will have to travel for your education.
- There is significantly less financial aid available for graduate study, and much of what does exist is set up for full-time study only.
- Although this attitude is beginning to change, reentry women have not always been viewed seriously as potential candidates for graduate school, and therefore little effort has been made to recruit them.
- Graduate departments are often more selective than undergraduate departments in choosing students, and the criteria for selection may inadvertently discriminate against students who have interrupted their education for a long time (for instance, by requiring prerequisite courses that have been offered only in the last five years).
- Graduate programs usually accept fewer transfer credits and may place limits on how long ago transferable credits can have been earned. Also, they place heavy importance on letters of recommendation from former professors as a criterion for admission. Many reentry students out of school for ten years or more may find it hard to obtain those letters.

While many graduate schools have given up requiring the Graduate Record Examinations (GRE) as a criterion for admission, some, especially the more prestigious ones, still use them. Find out whether or not you need to take them and what scores are considered the norm for admission to the school you're thinking about. Some schools will also require you to take a Subject Test in a specific area. These are given on the same day and in the same place as the GRE.

When choosing graduate schools, one thing to ask yourself is the amount of importance you want to place on attending a "name" school. Certainly, if you're going to be a doctor or a lawyer or a businesswoman, the fact that you graduated from Harvard will go a long way toward getting you a better-paid job. On the other hand, you will *need* a better-paid job to attend a "name" school, because it will usually cost you twice as much as attending the state university.

In graduate school, equally as valuable as the education you get are the people you meet. Graduate study is much more vocationally oriented than the typical undergraduate program. Students spend anywhere from eighteen months to seven or more years (in the case of some doctoral study) in the same program with others who will eventually be working in the same field. Especially for women, who have not yet developed the kind of "old-boy network" that spells career advancement, graduate study is a wonderful opportunity to meet people and make connections.

For further information on choosing a graduate school, consult the relevant volume of *Peterson's Annual Guides to Graduate Study* (Peterson's, Princeton, New Jersey), *The Courman Report* (National Educational Standards, Indianapolis), or *Guide to American Graduate Schools* by Harold R. Doughty (Penguin, New York). If you feel you need help preparing for the GRE, a good book to consider is *GRE—Expert Help for Higher Scores* by Thomas Martinson and Gino Crocetti (Arco, New York). For information about graduate financial aid, see publications listed in Appendix F and *The Graduate Scholarship Book* by Daniel Cassidy (Prentice Hall, Englewood Cliffs, New Jersey).

Training and Vocational Schools

The U.S. Department of Labor estimates that through 1995, the majority of jobs will require some degree of trade or technical training. If your major reason for going back to school is getting a job or moving up in the one you already have, then you may want to consider a licensed trade school or a technical school instead of a college.

Fastest-Growing Jobs, 1985–95

Occupation	Total Jobs Added	Percentage of Increase
Paralegal	104,000	98
Computer programmer	586,000	72
Computer systems analyst	520,000	69
Medical assistant	207,000	62
Data processing equipment repairer	78,000	56
Electrical engineer	597,000	53
Electrical technician	607,000	51
Computer operator	353,000	46
Operator of peripheral data processing equipment	102,000	45
Travel agent	103,000	44
Health-service manager	147,000	44
Physical therapist	25,000	42
Physician's assistant	10,000	40

Source: Occupational Outlook Quarterly, Bureau of Labor Statistics, Spring 1986.

The progress of thirteen of the fastest-growing jobs is charted above. In the case of almost every job listed, it is possible to gain the necessary skills either by going to college (most likely in a certificate program or an associate degree program at a two-year college) or by attending a training program at one of the more than 10,000 nationally approved private trade and technical schools.

According to the National Association of Trade and Technical Schools, training time for most jobs is anywhere from six months to two years. The following table gives some examples of the length of training time for an assortment of jobs.

───── Training Time for Selected Jobs ─────

Skill	Time (in wks.)	Skill	Time (in wks.)
Bank teller	32	Legal assistant/paralegal	24–52
Cardiac technician	12–48	Makeup artist	8–52
Computer operator	24–32	Massage therapist	52
Culinary arts worker	26–52	Medical assistant	12–48
Dental assistant	12–50	Photographer	12–150
Electrician	21–104	Printer	24–72
Emergency medical		Programmer analyst	34–208
technician	28–34	Real estate agent	6
Fashion		Respiratory therapist	26–52
illustrator	33–96	Surgical technician	52
Food service		Surveyor	15–72
specialist	52	Theater production	
Interior designer	64–108	specialist	60

Source: National Association of Trade and Technical Schools, 1989.

If, after carefully surveying the options, you're still not sure whether a career in the trades is right for you, take some time to think about the issues in the following sections.

Career Direction

Do you enjoy helping people, working with your hands, working with numbers, creating things, designing things, being outdoors? Identify your likes and dislikes, and then translate them into career possibilities, such as theater, dress design, allied health professions, electronic technology, advertising, or computer programming. The most important factor in making a career decision is choosing something you *like* to do.

Salary

What is the starting salary of the career you're considering? What can you expect to earn after two or three years on the job? What about after ten years? The following table shows average 1988 weekly earnings for full-time waged and salaried workers in the various categories of employment in the trades. Note the difference between men's and women's salaries, and keep that in mind as you make your decision.

Median Weekly Earnings, 1988

Occupation	Women	Men	Women's Earnings as a % of Men's
Managerial and professional specialty	$465	$666	69.8
Executive, administrative, and managerial occupations	430	682	63.0
Professional specialty	485	651	74.5
Technical, sales, and administrative support	305	472	64.6
Technicians and related support	384	510	75.3
Sales occupations	264	488	54.1
Administrative support, including clerical	305	418	73.0
Service occupations	208	299	69.6
Precision production, craft, and repair	302	446	67.7
Operators, fabricators, and laborers	238	352	67.6
Farming, forestry, and fishing	201	234	85.9

Source: U.S. Department of Labor, Women's Bureau, May 1989.

Advancement

Is the career you've chosen open-ended? Where can you go with it? If your goal is eventually to start your own business, will this career allow you that opportunity? How are women treated in this career? How many women move up in the organization? What will you need to do in order to advance?

Job Demand

Is there a need for your career specialty? How many jobs are available in this field? Are there more jobs than people wanting them or the other way around? Also, get a long-range projection of demand from the Bureau of Labor Statistics (212-337-2400). Make sure your job won't become obsolete in a few years.

Job Mobility

Where are the jobs? Are they in your area? Will you have to commute? What will your commute cost in terms of mileage and time? Will you have to travel? If so, how much? Can you request travel if it's what you want?

Working Conditions

What kind of benefits does the job offer? Is there paid maternity leave? What happens if your child gets sick? Does the company offer day care on the premises or provide low-cost day care nearby? What is the policy with regard to smoking? Check the health-care plan.

Advantages of Career Schools

Career schools offer many advantages to the student seeking specific job training. For one thing, they operate on a year-round basis, and most programs are run several times a year. Classes usually meet five days a week, although evening classes are almost always available.

While tuition can run from hundreds to thousands of dollars, depending on the program, the cost is usually far lower than that of going to college, since most training is over in a year or less. And financial aid is available from federal, state, and private agencies if you choose a school that is approved (which, given the consistently bad press given to vocational schools that are not approved, is the only kind of school you should be considering in the first place). Also, most schools will help you find a part-time apprenticeship in your field of study if you need more tuition assistance.

Classes in career schools are usually smaller than those in college, because of the importance of hands-on training. Most class time is spent in joblike settings where students solve problems that are directly related to the work they will be doing. Unlike the theoretical experience of most college professors, instructors in trade and technical schools have worked in their field. Their knowledge of the job is firsthand, and their approach to the subject is usually much more pragmatic.

Finally, career schools offer job-placement services and training in such skills as resume writing and interview techniques.

For more information on licensed career schools, write to the National Association of Trade and Technical Schools, Department CS, P.O. Box 10429, Rockville, MD 20850. Ask for the *Handbook of Private Accredited Trade and Technical Schools,* which has both a national directory of schools and a list of ninety-eight careers.

Chapter

4

Nontraditional Options for Degree Study

How would you like to get a college degree without ever sitting in a classroom? How about getting one by going to school only every other weekend? How about a degree program with a course of study designed totally by you?

The above are only a few of the growing number of nontraditional educational options available to the adult learner. In this chapter, you will read about a few others, all of them equally valid and equally accepted, and all of them alternatives to what we've always thought of as the *only* way to go to school.

Credit by Examination

Let's say you're thinking about going back to school to study information technology. Let's also say that for the past five years you've been working as a salesperson in a store that sells computers. Now you look in the catalog of courses you will be required to take and see one called Introduction to Computers. Everything in the course description sounds like information you think you already know. Do you have to take this course?

Not if you "test out" of it. If you think you have a particular level of proficiency in *any* subject area, you can save a lot of time and money by simply taking a test in it and, if you score well enough, gaining exemption from having to take that subject in school. According to a 1986 survey by the American Council on Education's Higher Education Panel, 93 percent of the nation's colleges and universities grant credit by examination.

The most commonly used tests for obtaining credit are the College-Level Examination Program (CLEP) exams developed by the College Board. There are two kinds of CLEP tests:

1. General exams, which let you earn anywhere from 3 to 6 credits in courses that most students take as first- or second-year requirements. The areas you can choose to be tested in are humanities, natural sciences, social sciences, mathematics, and English composition.
2. Subject exams, given in thirty different areas, which let you earn credit for individual undergraduate courses. Subject exams require a higher degree of specialized knowledge and training than the general examinations and are a good bet only if you have gained specific knowledge or skills from your job experience or have done outside course work or independent reading in a particular area.

CLEP exams are held during the third week of every month at more than 1,000 centers throughout the country. Each type of exam currently costs $37 and consists of multiple-choice and some essay questions. The tests are scored by the College Board, but it is up to the individual schools to determine what constitutes a passing grade for each CLEP exam. This is done in order to allow schools that offer credit by examination to maintain their own standards of quality. Students who want to improve their scores must wait six months before repeating a CLEP test.

For more information on which colleges near you accept CLEP credit, write to CLEP, Box 6601, Princeton, NJ 08541-6601, for a list of the over 2,000 participating colleges. The College Board also has a guide that gives a description of each test offered by CLEP and a number of practice sheets so that you can familiarize yourself with the testing format. This guide is available from College Board Publications, Department B10, Box 886, New York, NY 10101-0886.

In addition to CLEP, the American College Testing Program offers a group of standardized tests through its Proficiency Examination Program (PEP). Like CLEP, PEP tests both general knowledge and individual subject areas. For information about PEP, write to the American College Testing Program, Proficiency Examination Program, Box 168, Iowa City, IA 52240.

New York State has its own credit-by-examination program, the College Proficiency Examination Program (CPEP). For information, write to the New York State Education Department, Office on Noncollegiate Sponsored Instruction, 99 Washington Avenue, Albany, NY 12230. Other states also have their own program, including Ohio (the Ohio University Examination Program) and New Jersey (the Thomas A. Edison State College Examination Program). Information about these programs can be obtained through state education offices, which are usually located in the state capital.

Flexible Scheduling

One of the most obvious indicators of a school's commitment to its adult population is whether it has flexible scheduling or not. Since seven out of every ten reentry students work full-time, a school can expect to benefit from adult enrollment dollars only if classes are scheduled in slots other than the traditional 9 to 5.

Topping the list of alternative schedules specifically geared toward adults is the concept of the "weekend college." In the last few years, the number of schools offering such programs has more than doubled.

While every school's description of "weekend" varies, most run classes on Friday nights and on Saturday and Sunday mornings and afternoons. Classes are typically 3 to 4 hours long, and a "semester" consists of attendance every other weekend for four or five months. Weekend students intent on getting a degree in four years usually have to spend anywhere from 9 to 12 hours every other weekend year-round for the full four years.

Understandably, most weekend programs are geared toward working people seeking to make career changes. Degrees offered, therefore, are generally occupationally oriented ones such as business administration, nursing, and communications. It is rare to find weekend colleges offering degree study in British history or metaphysical philosophy, for example.

On a more traditional plane are night classes, which have long been standard offerings at most schools. A few schools, however, have recently taken the concept of "night" a little further than was envisioned previously. At Maricopa Community College, which has seven campuses scattered throughout Maricopa County in Arizona, not only can standard night classes run until 11 p.m. or later, but some actually start at midnight!

And then there's the increasing number of early-morning programs. At the University of Northern Colorado, for example, many classes start at 7 a.m. At Long Island University's C. W. Post Campus, starting time for some classes is—are you ready?—6 a.m.!

External Degree Programs

Despite the existence of alternative scheduling options, you still might not be able to attend class on campus. It may be that your job or family responsibilities make it hard for you to be away for any length of time, or the distance may be just too great for you to travel it on a regular basis.

It may also be that the kind of study you want to do falls between subject areas, as in the case of someone who eventually wants to use physical education as a counseling tool. Such a person could either take a dual major in a traditional college program—a practice that, while steadily gaining in acceptance, is still frowned upon by some department heads—or choose an external degree program that allows her to design her own course of study. In some cases, external-degree students opt to major in areas that are not even available for college credit, such as recreation therapy or food design.

By definition, an external degree is one that is earned primarily off campus without classroom instruction. These programs employ what's called self-directed study, with faculty members acting as advisers rather than instructors. The total amount of time spent on campus in such programs varies from no time at all to a few weeks, depending on the school. While there are a great many accredited undergraduate schools offering external degree programs, there are only a few accredited schools offering such programs at the graduate level.

To earn an external degree, you will first have to draw up a "learning contract" with the adviser who will be your main contact throughout your course of study. Such a contract will specify:

1. The number of credits you have been awarded for previous experience or study.
2. The number of requirements you still have to meet in order to get the degree.
3. How you will satisfy those requirements.

Such contracts reflect a blending of your particular educational wants and needs with what your adviser determines will satisfy the requirements of the college.

For example, here is a contract drawn up for a student choosing to pursue an external Bachelor of Science degree in business management:

Credits needed to graduate: 120
Transfer credits granted: 80
Exam (CLEP) credits granted: 15
Portfolio assessment credits granted (see subsequent paragraphs): 10

Plan for earning remaining 15 credits:
- 3 credits in business law through correspondence course
- 6 credits in operations management through computer-facilitated learning (discussed later in chapter)
- 6 credits in transportation management through guided independent study

The actual course work you still have to do after having been awarded the maximum number of credits for previous learning may be divided into separate assignments, as in the preceding listing, or may be grouped together into larger units of learning. For example, you may be able to get a 15-credit block for an extended period of study of computers and data processing. Depending on your major, you will be expected to do varying amounts of reading, research, or writing. A counseling student, for example, may be required to read certain books on therapeutic approaches, turn in certain progress reports in the form of papers and case studies, and present a final project, possibly detailing a three- or four-month period of actual counseling of clients.

In an external degree program, each person works at her own pace, so the amount of time it takes to earn a degree varies anywhere from six months to four years (find out whether the school you're considering has a time limit). Most schools use the portfolio assessment process when awarding credit for previous life experience. Most also give credit for CLEP or other standardized exams, previously completed training or certificate programs, and correspondence courses.

Empire State College was the first public college devoted entirely to external degrees to receive regional accreditation. Located within the huge State University of New York system, Empire State is a consortium of forty-five tiny campuses, some no bigger than a small building, scattered throughout the state. With an average student age of 37, it caters almost exclusively to adult learners.

Empire State has an unusually liberal policy of granting credit for prior learning. Between transfer credits from other schools and credit for prior learning, the average B.A. candidate at Empire State has earned 82 of the 128 credits needed for graduation before even starting the program. The maximum number of credits possible for prior experience is 96. In the case of associate degrees, the typical candidate can earn up to 40 of the required 64 credits on the basis of prior experience.

At Empire State, credit for prior learning is awarded for what was *gained* from an educational experience; in other words, no credit is awarded for the experience itself unless the student can prove something was learned from it that is considered college-level education. A candidate may, for example, have spent the past ten years working in an office setting. Unless she can *prove* that she learned something specific about data processing or information management, she will not be awarded college credit simply on the assumption that she must have learned these things.

For further information on the Empire State College program, contact State University of New York Empire State College, 2 Union Avenue, Saratoga Springs, NY 12866 (518-587-2100).

The awarding of credit for prior learning at Empire State and most other colleges offering external degree programs takes place through assessment of the portfolio, a three-part document:

1. **A course description.** Students usually look at traditional college catalogs to find a course whose content sounds most like what they know from experience. A student studying for an external degree in human and social services, for example, may see a course called Health and Nutrition. Having worked as a dietitian in a hospital setting for fifteen years, she thinks she knows most of what the catalog says will be taught in that class. She copies the complete course description.

2. **A narrative.** In this section, the student discusses her knowledge in the area of health and nutrition, specifically as it relates to the course description just mentioned. If, for example, the course will cover acids and alkalies, she lists how and where she has learned about them already. She lists any training received, formal or otherwise; any personal study or readings in the area; any workshops or seminars attended; and any other experience she feels may have been important in learning about acids and alkalies. The narrative should detail not only how she learned about them but how long it took, what methods were used, what texts or manuals she read on the subject, whether she was ever supervised by anybody while learning, and how this supervisor evaluated whether she actually completed the learning or not.

3. **Evidence.** This section should provide comprehensive documentation of the knowledge claimed in the narrative. This can include official transcripts, letters, official outlines, the student's own notebooks, reports done and graded, copies of licensure requirements—whatever would

serve to convince a portfolio assessor that, in fact, the learning claimed by the student had taken place.

Portfolios generally take anywhere from two to six weeks to be evaluated, and they are usually decided upon by an assessment team composed either partially or entirely of faculty members. Appendix A lists a number of tips from the American Council on Education on how best to gain acceptance for portfolio credits.

Like Empire State College, Thomas A. Edison State College in New Jersey is part of a large state university system. Also like Empire State, Edison does not offer classroom instruction, specializing instead in the evaluation of learning. At Edison, students working toward either an associate or bachelor's degree go through a three-step process:

1. **Evaluation of existing credits.** At Edison, the only acceptable avenues for the outright awarding of prior-learning credit are transfer credit, exam credit, approved licenses and certificates, and approved training programs.
2. **Portfolio assessment.** Like Empire State, Edison does not award credit for an experience itself, only for learning that took place as a result of that experience. Portfolios are prepared showing the learning the student thinks took place while she was a homemaker or a bank teller or the operator of a word processor. At Edison, there is no limit to the number of credits students can earn for their portfolio.
3. **Completing the program.** Once the student has gained all the advance credit possible, a learning plan for earning the rest of the credits needed to complete the degree is formulated. Methods that can be drawn upon include independent study, approved training programs, guided study, computer-facilitated learning, correspondence courses, and classroom courses offered by other schools.

For further information on Edison's programs, contact Thomas A. Edison State College, 101 West State Street, CN 545, Trenton, NJ 08625 (609-984-1150).

While such external degree programs as Empire State's or Edison's (or the University of Maryland's University College or Norwich University's Vermont College) may sound tremendously appealing in that you never have to go to class, there are a number of considerations worth mulling over before making a decision.

First of all, you should know if the program is accredited. This is important, especially if you will need either federal or state financial aid, which is available only for study in programs that have received or are about to receive accreditation. For more information on the schools offering external degree programs, consult *Bear's Guide to Nontraditional Education* (Ten Speed Press, Berkeley).

Ask yourself if you are a self-motivated, self-disciplining kind of person. Can you handle designing your own program, determining what to do and when, sticking to a self-devised timetable? While your relationship with your adviser most likely will be a close one, what you do, how you do it, and when you do it will all be up to you.

Do you have the necessary resources to put together a self-directed program? You undoubtedly will need access to libraries and research services, mentors to supervise each of your unit projects, and proximity to people in the field who can guide you to what's available and where.

Do you communicate well in writing? Since you will not be attending classes, most of the communication between you and your adviser will be written. From your initial learning contract to the dozens of reports and papers detailing what you're learning, your progress will be measured on the strength of how well you present it in writing.

Are you prepared to forgo the social aspect of attending class? Many women who go back to school talk about the support they received from other students as having been crucial to their success. In an external degree program, you will have neither the opinions of other students to balance your own nor the network of friends and contacts one usually makes while in a traditional school setting.

Do you know enough about your intended field to know what should be included in a course of study? While your adviser might be familiar with certain aspects, it will be up to you to design a full-fledged program. Look for schools that offer a program in your proposed field of study, and check their catalogs to see what courses have been included.

Are you considering an external degree program only because you think it would be easier than a more traditional one? If so, you might want to think it through a little more before enrolling. External degree programs are accredited by the same agencies as traditional ones. As such, they are subject to the same stringent proofs of their validity. In addition, they are constantly being challenged by those who place them in the same category as the infamous "diploma mills." In most cases, external degree programs wind up demanding more of their students than traditional programs in order to "prove" their legitimacy. Some may be easier than others to get through, but don't let this be your sole criterion for choosing to go the external degree route.

Computer-Facilitated Learning

To an increasing number of students, going to school means having to travel no further than the nearest computer terminal or video monitor. Via the very latest in telecommunications wizardry, it is now possible to study for anything from an undergraduate degree in liberal arts to a Master of Arts in computer studies to a few courses' worth of information on stress management.

While there are at present fewer than a dozen or so "on-line universities" delivering such courses, estimates put the number of students enrolled in electronic degree programs in the tens of thousands. Most programs are still linked to traditional colleges and universities that have the necessary authority to grant credit and degrees. Some, however, are themselves fully accredited and, as such, are able to provide their students with the same possibilities for federal and state financial aid as any other accredited institution. A few have established ties with major corporations, providing both the resources necessary to augment the learning and a ready pool of people who can study for an entire degree program at their video monitor during working hours—all on the company payroll!

All of the currently operating electronic universities can trace their beginnings to 1981. At that time, the Annenberg School of Communications agreed to provide the Corporation for Public Broadcasting with $10-million a year for fifteen years. The purpose, as stated in the *New York Times*, was to ". . . develop flexible and innovative educational approaches more in keeping with shifting national demographics that now find 30 percent of the student population older than 24, and more than 40 percent attending college part time."

One of the first programs to benefit from the Annenberg award was the Center for Open Learning (COL) and station WYCC-TV in Chicago. Operated by the Media Programs Department of Chicago Citywide College, COL offers an assortment of nontraditional education options in the form of more than seventy-five different courses for college credit. Accounting, geology, physics, poetry, psychology, and an introduction to microcomputers are just a few of the courses available.

Programs can be watched by any Chicagoan who decides to tune in. Those who have paid to take the course for credit, however, receive a printed course package that includes reading and textbook assignments, course outlines from a faculty member, and regularly scheduled tests. Enrolled students can even have telephone conferences with instructors or in-person review sessions.

For more information on COL, contact Mark Martin, Director of Operations, The Center for Open Learning, 226 West Jackson Boulevard, Chicago, IL 60606-6997 (312-855-8213).

A more highly packaged system is available through the National Technological University (NTU), operating out of Fort Collins, Colorado, and catering to graduate students only. Its services are geared for on-the-job engineers and other technical professionals, and instruction is delivered to the job site by satellite transmission and videotape. NTU offers 455 courses leading to Master of Science degrees in computer science, computer engineering, management, electrical engineering, engineering management, and manufacturing systems engineering. Eighteen percent of its students are women.

Currently, twenty-nine universities make up NTU's degree-granting consortium (among them Iowa State, Boston University, Purdue, the University of Arizona, Notre Dame, and Michigan Technological University). Its network of sponsoring sites has grown to include over 200 locations, including offices of AT&T, Digital Equipment Corporation, Eastman Kodak, IBM, and NCR. NTU recently added nine new satellite linkups, increasing its delivery capacity to more than 8,000 hours of instruction, some of it for credit and some of it not.

For more information about NTU, contact Douglas M. Yeager, National Technological University, P.O. Box 700, Fort Collins, CO 80522 (303-484-6050).

While NTU deals in graduate study only, American Open University (AOU), a division of New York Institute of Technology, presents students with an opportunity to get an undergraduate degree without leaving the house or office. The Bachelor of Science degree is offered in behavioral science, business administration, and general studies. Courses cost $255 (half the price of taking them on campus) and are transmitted through a computer network that can reach anywhere in the world where there is a computer, a modem, and a telephone. One interesting thing about AOU is that students taking electronic courses can interact with both a mentor who directs the seminar discussions and other students taking the seminar at the same time.

For further information on AOU, contact Andrew Sass, Director, American Open University of the New York Institute of Technology, Central Islip, NY 11722 (out of state, 800-222-NYIT; in state, 516-348-3300).

Connected Education, Inc., operates in much the same fashion as AOU, but with a greater range of subject matter in both academics and areas of personal enrichment. It operates in conjunction with the New School of Social Research in New York, through which it offers an M.A. program in media studies, and with the Brooklyn Campus of Polytechnic University, through which it offers over fifty graduate-level courses ranging from Introduction to Software Documentation to Professional Management Ethics.

In addition to over 1,000 listed course offerings, Connect-Ed can provide tailor-made courses as part of what it calls "professional fulfillment." For example, it has created an entire module in business and scholarly writing for a woman in Utah who needed to put together a book proposal. But that's not all. As part of its desire to be first among electronic universities, Connect-Ed offers an on-line library, an electronic book-ordering service, and the Connect-Ed Cafe, for all the gossip and intellectual chitchat that's part of any typical campus coffeehouse.

For more information, contact Paul Levinson, Director, Connected Education, Inc., Suite 6F, 92 Van Cortland Parkway South, Bronx, NY 10463 (212-549-6509).

And then there's the huge San Francisco–based Electronic University Network (EUN), which offers undergraduate degrees in affiliation with Thomas A. Edison State College in New Jersey and the State University of New York Regents Program, and graduate degrees in affiliation with Saginaw Valley State University in Michigan and John F. Kennedy University in Orinda, California. Currently, 8,000 students are enrolled, participating in courses by way of personal computer and communicating one-to-one with instructors over electronic mail systems.

Over thirty-five Fortune 500 companies — among them AT&T, Clorox, NYNEX, PacBell, and Federal Express — now include EUN in their educational and tuition-reimbursement programs. Participants can take courses leading to degrees in business, natural sciences, mathematics, social sciences, and the humanities. In addition, there is an eclectic menu of special on-line items, including Stress Management, Bioethical Problems in Biology, and Introduction to Paralegalism.

For further information on EUN, contact the Office of Admissions, Electronic University Network, 385 8th Street, San Francisco, CA 94103 (415-552-6000).

While most of the organizations mentioned thus far use personal computers to transmit course work, Mind Extension University (MEU) uses a national cable channel to televise hundreds of courses that range from Library Science to The Age of Enlightenment. The price of each course is $300, with books and materials running from $50 to $100 per course. Courses are accepted for credit by over fifteen colleges and universities, the State University of New York and the University of South Carolina among them. MEU also offers a program leading to a Master of Business Administration degree through Colorado State Unversity, as well as self-directed continuing education and personal-enrichment programs. All courses are available 24 hours a day on MEU-affiliated cable systems and on satellite broadcasts.

For more information, contact Mind Extension University, 9697 East Mineral Avenue, Englewood, CO 80112 (800-777-MIND).

Finally, there's CorpNet, a corporate-training network for on-site delivery of University of Nebraska courses and workshops. The CorpNet system utilizes one-way video and two-way audio connections that allow participants in dozens of corporations to interact with instructors teaching actual classes at the university, as well as with their on- and off-campus classmates. Students in office settings hundreds of miles away can ask questions, offer comments, and take an active role in the class while it is going on.

Through CorpNet, students can pursue a graduate program in engineering, advance through an undergraduate degree program by taking selected business or engineering courses, or earn a certificate in business principles and management techniques by taking advanced management seminars. For more information, call Nancy Aden, Program Specialist, at 402-472-1924.

Correspondence Courses

Home-study courses have always suffered from their association in people's minds with the matchbook covers exhorting you to "Send today for information on how to get a degree through the mail. No work. No requirements." While, sadly, such educational frauds still exist, there are a number of correspondence schools that offer perfectly legitimate education opportunities for students whose schedules do not allow traditional study or even most forms of nontraditional study. The key, once again, is accreditation.

Appendix B provides a partial list of nationally accredited correspondence schools. For a more complete listing, the National University Continuing Education Association (NUCEA) publishes *The Independent Study Catalog: NUCEA's Guide to Independent Study Through Correspondence Instruction* (Peterson's, Princeton, New Jersey). It contains the names, addresses, and course offerings at over seventy colleges and universities.

If you are thinking of applying such credit toward a degree program, however, check with your intended college to establish the number of credits it will allow you to take through correspondence. Most colleges impose severe limits.

Chapter

5

How to Pay for Your Education

Audrey Bresson has been working as an administrative assistant for the past twelve years. Recently she applied for promotion to a supervisory position and was told that, despite the hundreds of new employees she has trained over the years, she would have to go back to school to earn a college degree before she could be considered for a management position. Audrey felt that, with two sons in college and a daughter in high school, it would be too much of a strain on the family budget for her to enroll in a degree program. Then last week Audrey found out that her company had both a time-release program and a tuition-reimbursement plan for those taking job-related training. Although technically the program was open to any employee, only management-level employees were taking advantage of it.

Sheila Lawston completed two years of college right after graduating from high school in 1958. Now she would like to finish her bachelor's degree work and maybe even go on to graduate study in psychology, but she doesn't have the money to pay for college. Sheila assumed she wouldn't be eligible for financial aid because she would only be attending part-time and because she makes over $17,000 a year. However, when her friend, also a reentry student, suggested that she talk to an admissions counselor, Sheila found out that, with recent changes in the financial aid legislation, she was probably eligible for substantial federal, state, and institutional aid.

Edie Valera, 51, was recently divorced after thirty-two years of marriage. With two children grown and out of the house, Edie knows she needs to get a job, not only to save her sanity but also to provide herself with sorely needed income. After a number of unsuccessful interviews, however, she has realized that employers are reluctant to hire a woman who doesn't have a college degree and hasn't held a job since her husband finished law school twenty-six years ago. While she'd like to go back to school, she knows she can't afford to pay the steep tuition fees she remembers from her children's college years. Yesterday, Edie's neighbor stopped by with a special financial aid bulletin for reentry women that she'd picked up at the bank. It talked about low-interest loans, as well as special "reentry scholarships" funded by a consortium of community organizations.

Wendy Miller is clearly eligible for need-based aid (from either federal, state, or institutional sources) due both to her low income and to the fact that she's a single parent caring for two preschool children. She hasn't applied, however, because she has always heard that only full-time students were eligible for financial aid, and she only takes one or two courses a semester. While meeting with her adviser on another matter, Wendy mentioned that she'd have to skip summer semester because she didn't have the money to pay for tuition. Her adviser told her about federal financial aid for half-time students (taking 6 hours a semester) and about the special aid program set up by the college for students who were less than half-time.

Like the four women just mentioned, many reentry students assume that they're not eligible for financial aid or that, if they are, it won't be enough. Ten years ago, they would have been right. Today, however, things have changed—drastically! Currently, more than 60 percent of the students involved in postsecondary education receive some kind of financial aid, whether they are 17 or 47 and whether they take 18 or 3 credits per semester.

"The money's there," says Elinor Azenberg, Director of Reentry Programs at New York University. "It's just a question of whether or not you want to put in the research time necessary to find out how to get it." The more you're willing to look, says Azenberg, the better your chances of putting together a financial aid program that will cover your educational costs.

In this chapter, you will learn not only about what's available in terms of federal, state, and private money but also about where and how to find the amount of money you need. Remember, the money is there. You just have to believe you can get it and look hard enough.

Where to Find Information

Public Libraries

A wealth of information is available at the nearest library in the form of dozens of reference books listing sources of private and public financial support. Granted, it's no fun looking through hundreds of pages of who offers what. But remember that most people are going to feel exactly the way you feel about this kind of research—"I don't want to do it." This will cut down the competition significantly. If you take your time and copy down the names of fifteen or twenty companies offering scholarship support, you should eventually hit on one that will work for you. (Since it takes time to sift through all the material, send for guidelines, and file an application for aid, you should start a library search well in advance of the time you will actually need the money.)

Also, if you plan to attend school outside your local area, the library will have various directories that list the addresses of specific schools, so that you can contact admissions and financial aid offices directly.

Women's Organizations

Groups such as the YWCA, women's centers, women's clubs, local displaced homemaker centers, and women's chapters of professional societies often can provide information about financial aid opportunities. Some even offer their own workshops and courses on how to word your application for aid in a way that increases your chances of being noticed.

State or County Commissions on Women

If there is such an organization in your area, its staff may be able to tell you about financial aid opportunities for women in your locality and where to go to get more information. State commissions on women are usually located in the state capital.

Military-Based Education Offices

If you are in the military yourself or are part of a servicemember's family, the education officer at the nearest base can provide many kinds of information regarding financial aid opportunities. The military's most-used form of assistance is the G.I. bill.

Campus-Based Services

In addition to inquiring at the financial aid office on your campus, you should check at the career planning and placement office for information about jobs that offer tuition-assistance benefits; at the reentry students' office (most schools have them), which may have special listings of financial aid available specifically for reentry women; and at the child-care center (available on more and more campuses), where you can find out about the availability of low-cost or no-cost day care (financial aid, remember, comes in many forms).

Federal Financial Aid

More than 8,000 colleges, universities, hospital schools of nursing, and vocational and technical schools take part in the U.S. Department of Education's financial aid programs. In order to be eligible for federal money, which can be used only for expenses related to attending school, you must first meet the following requirements:

- You must be enrolled as a regular student in an eligible program.
- You must be a U.S. citizen or an eligible noncitizen.
- You must show that you have financial need. Most federal student aid is awarded on the basis of need. A standard formula is used to determine the amount of aid, but in general it is based on the difference between the cost of your education (tuition, fees, room, board, books, supplies, and related expenses) and the amount you and your family are expected to contribute.
- You must make satisfactory progress in your course of study.
- You must neither be in default nor owe a refund for any federal aid you have received in the past.
- You must have a high school diploma or its equivalent as established by your score on the General Educational Development (GED) test. If you have neither diploma nor GED, you must pass a standardized admissions test that measures your aptitude to complete your course of study successfully or enroll in and successfully complete a remedial program required by the school and not exceeding one academic year in length.
- You must be enrolled at least half-time (6 semester hours) to receive a Pell Grant, a Perkins Loan, or an SLS loan.

Having met all the above criteria, you must next file an application. This is a two-step process consisting of the following:

1. You file an Application for Federal Student Aid. This application is available at any institutional financial aid office or by request from the Federal Student Aid Information Center at 800-333-INFO. The deadline for filing the application is usually May 1. It will take four to six weeks for your application to be processed, and if it's sent back for confirmation or correction, it will take another two to three weeks to reprocess it (so *be careful* when you fill it out).

2. Four to six weeks after you apply for federal student aid, you'll receive a Student Aid Report (SAR). The SAR will contain the information you gave on your application plus two numbers that tell you about your eligibility for federal student aid: the Student Aid Index (SAI), which determines your Pell Grant eligibility (more on this later), and your Family Contribution number, which tells how much you and your family will be expected to contribute toward the cost of your education. This second number also will be used in determining your eligibility for the campus-based and Stafford Loan programs, which will be described later. If your SAR says you're eligible for a Pell Grant, you will have about a month to fill in the extra information requested. If your SAR says you're not eligible for a Pell Grant, you should contact the financial aid officer at your school to discuss alternatives.

Although the process of determining a student's eligibility for federal student aid is generally the same for all applicants, there is some flexibility. For example, if you indicate on the application that either you or your spouse is a dislocated worker or displaced homemaker, special consideration will be given to your financial status. Also, certain applicants with incomes of less than $15,000 can skip many of the questions on the application form.

In some cases, your situation will warrant special attention. You may, for example, expect a drastic reduction in your future income due to separation or divorce, a spouse's death, or loss of a full-time job. If so, you should see your financial aid officer, who will explain what steps to take. In the above situation—change in income status—he or she might instruct you to fill out the form with your estimated income for the coming year instead of your actual income. Application forms for any of the federally funded financial aid programs can be found at the financial aid office of the school you're planning to attend or at your local library. You can also call the Federal Student Aid Information Center Hotline at 800-333-INFO. The Information Center also can help with:

- Filing a financial aid application or correcting an SAR.
- Checking on whether a school takes part in federal aid programs.
- Understanding student eligibility requirements.
- Understanding the process by which financial aid awards are determined.
- Directing your complaints to the right office.
- Understanding the verification process (the Department of Education or your school may require you to *prove* that what you reported on your application is correct).
- Understanding general financial aid program requirements.

The Information Center *cannot* help you, however, if you want to find out whether your application has been processed or if you want a duplicate SAR. To make these requests, call the Federal Application Processing Center, 319-337-3738.

The following table lays out the six federal financial aid programs for students. The programs are decribed in detail in subsequent sections.

Federal Financial Aid Programs

Program	Who Is Eligible?	Amount Available	Type of Aid
Pell Grant	Undergraduates	$2,300 maximum	Grant
Supplemental Educational Opportunity Grant	Undergraduates	$4,000 maximum	Grant
College Work-Study	Undergraduates and graduate students	Varies	Salary for work done
Perkins Loan	Undergraduates and graduate students	$4,500–$9,000 for undergraduates; up to $18,000 for graduate students	Loan
Stafford Loan	Undergraduates and graduate students	$2,625–$4,000 for undergraduates; up to $7,500 for graduate students	Loan
Supplemental Loans for Students	Undergraduates and graduate students	$4,000–$20,000	Loan

The Pell Grant Program

Pell Grants are awarded to undergraduates only and don't have to be repaid. The maximum award is $2300 at the time of this writing; how much of that you actually get depends on your need. For many students, Pell Grants provide a "foundation" of financial aid to which aid from other federal and nonfederal sources can be added. Eligibility is limited to five full years of undergraduate study toward a first baccalaureate or professional degree. You may, however, receive a Pell Grant for a sixth year if you're enrolled in a program that takes more than four years to complete. Your school may also waive the time limit if you become ill or are injured, if a relative dies, or in cases of individual hardship.

To determine if you're eligible for a Pell Grant, the Department of Education uses a standard formula to evaluate the information you report on your application for student aid. The formula produces the Student Aid Index number. If your number is low enough, you're eligible; the lower the number, the larger the amount of the award. If you want to determine your own SAI without waiting four to six weeks for your SAR, you can perform the calculations yourself. Write to Formula Book, Department L-10, Pueblo, CO 81009-0015.

The deadline for filing applications is usually May 1. You will get written notification of whether you have received an award or not within four to six weeks of applying. If you have received an award, your school will credit the award to your account, pay you directly, or use a combination of these two methods.

Campus-Based Programs

The Supplemental Educational Opportunity Grant (SEOG), College Work-Study (CWS), and Perkins Loan programs are referred to as campus based because they are administered by the financial aid office at each participating school. Although the programs are distinct, they have some elements in common:

- You can go to school less than half-time and still be eligible.
- How much aid you receive depends on your financial need, the amount of other aid you'll receive, and the availability of funds at your school. Campus-based programs are not like the Pell Grant Program, which provides funds to every eligible student. Each school participating in a campus-based program receives a certain amount of money to be distributed through that program. When the money is gone, there are no more awards from that program for that year.

- There is no single deadline for applying, as there is for the Pell Grant Program. Each school sets its own. Most deadlines, however, are usually early in the calendar year, usually earlier than for Pell Grants. Be sure to check with the financial aid office at the school you're planning to attend.

The Supplemental Educational Opportunity Grant Program

A Supplemental Educational Opportunity Grant is for undergraduates with exceptional financial need. Priority is given to Pell Grant recipients. You can get up to $4,000 a year, and the money does not have to be paid back.

As with Pell Grants, the school will credit your SEOG directly to your account, pay you directly, or use a combination of these two methods. Schools must pay students at least once per term, regardless of whether the year is divided into semesters, trimesters, or quarters.

The College Work-Study Program

The College Work-Study Program provides jobs for undergraduates and graduate students. Students are chosen on the basis of financial need and are paid according to the type of work they do and its level of difficulty. All recipients are paid at least the current federal minimum wage.

If you're an undergraduate, you'll be paid by the hour. If you're a graduate student, you'll either be paid by the hour or receive a salary. In either case, you will be paid at least once a month.

CWS jobs are either on or off campus. If you work on campus, you'll usually work for your school. If you work off campus, your job usually will involve work that is in the public interest, and your employer usually will be a private or public nonprofit organization or a local, state, or federal agency. Some schools, however, have agreements with private-sector employers for CWS jobs. Your work hours will be set by the school, and the amount you earn cannot exceed your CWS award.

The Perkins Loan Program

A Perkins Loan (formerly National Direct Student Loan) is a low-interest (5 percent) loan for both undergraduates and graduate students. It is made through the school's financial aid office. The school is your lender, and this loan must be repaid.

Depending on the circumstances, you may borrow:

- $4,500 if you're enrolled in a vocational program or if you have completed less than two years of a program leading to a bachelor's degree.

- $9,000 if you're an undergraduate student who has already completed two years of study toward a bachelor's degree and who has achieved third-year status. This total includes any amount you borrowed under the Perkins Loan Program for your first two years of study.
- $18,000 for graduate or professional study. This total includes any amount you borrowed under the Perkins Loan Program for your undergraduate study.

If you're at least a half-time student, you have a grace period of six months after you graduate, leave school, or drop below half-time status to begin repaying the loan. If you're less than half-time, your grace period may be different. Check with your financial aid administrator.

The amount of each repayment depends on the size of your debt and on the length of your repayment period. Usually, you will have to pay at least $30 a month. The table that follows shows typical monthly payments and total interest charges for three different 5-percent loans over a ten-year period.

Repayment of Perkins Loans

Total Indebtedness	Number of Payments	Monthly Payment	Total Interest Charges	Total Repaid
$ 4,500	120	$ 47.73	$1,227.60	$ 5,727.60
9,000	120	95.46	2,455.20	11,455.20
18,000	120	190.92	4,910.40	22,910.40

Source: U.S. Department of Education, 1989.

If you default on repayment of your Perkins Loan, your school can sue you to collect that amount, and it can even ask the federal government for help in collecting from you. The school or the federal government will notify credit bureaus of your default, and the IRS can withhold your tax refund, applying it instead toward repayment of your loan.

There are a few cases in which repayment of a Perkins Loan can be canceled:

- Part of your loan will be canceled for each complete academic year that you're a full-time teacher of handicapped children or for each complete academic year that you teach full-time in a designated elementary or secondary school serving low-income students. In both these cases, your entire loan will have been canceled after the fifth consecutive year of teaching. To find out which schools are designated, contact a student financial aid office.

- Part of your loan will be canceled for each year of full-time work in specified Head Start programs. After the seventh year, your entire loan will have been canceled.
- Up to 70 percent of your loan can be canceled for service as a Peace Corps or VISTA volunteer: 30 percent during the first two years and 40 percent during the next two years.
- If you serve as an enlisted person in certain selected specialties of the U.S. Army, the Army Reserve, the Army National Guard, or the Air National Guard, the Department of Defense will repay a portion of your loan as an enlistment incentive.

The Stafford Loan Program

This was formerly known as the Guaranteed Student Loan (GSL) Program. Stafford Loans are low-interest loans made by such lenders as banks, credit unions, or savings and loan associations. Sometimes a school acts as a lender. These loans are insured by the federal government and must be repaid.

For new borrowers (those with no previous Stafford or GSL loans), the current interest rate is 8 percent for the first four years and 10 percent after that. For those who currently have a GSL at 7, 8, or 9 percent, the interest rate for any future Stafford Loan remains 7, 8, or 9 percent.

Depending on your financial need, you may borrow up to:

- $2,625 a year if you're a first- or second-year undergraduate student.
- $4,000 a year if you have completed two years of study and have achieved third-year status.
- $7,500 a year if you're a graduate student.

The total outstanding Stafford Loan and GSL debt you can have as an undergraduate is $17,250. The total for graduate or professional study is $54,750, including any Stafford or GSL loans made at the undergraduate level.

You cannot borrow more than the cost of your education. If, for example, you're a first-year student whose cost of education is $4000 and you have a $1,500 Pell Grant, the maximum amount you can borrow on a Stafford Loan is $2,500.

Since not every lender participates in the Stafford Loan Program, you should start looking for one that does as soon as you know you're going back to school. After you submit your application to a lender, it usually takes four to six weeks to get your loan approved. In order to find out who the participating lenders are in your state, call the Federal Student Aid Information Center Hotline.

Repayment of Stafford Loans starts six months after you graduate, leave school, or drop below half-time status. The amount of each payment depends on the size of your debt and on the length of your repayment period. Usually, you'll have to pay at least $50 a month. The following table shows sample monthly payments and total interest charges for 8-percent loans of varying amounts.

Repayment of Stafford Loans

Total Indebtedness	Number of Payments	Monthly Payment	Total Interest Charges	Total Repaid
$ 2,500	60	$ 50.70	$ 541.46	$ 3,041.46
5,000	60	101.39	1,082.92	6,082.92
10,000	120	121.33	4,559.31	14,559.31
12,500	120	151.67	5,699.14	18,199.14
25,000	120	303.33	11,398.28	36,398.28

Source: U.S. Department of Education, 1989.

Stafford Loans can be canceled only if you serve as an enlisted person in one of the same defense specialties that apply to Perkins Loans. Under certain conditions, however, your loan payments can be deferred. Check with your lender for a list of these conditions.

Supplemental Loans for Students

This program provides additional funds for educational expenses. Like Stafford Loans, Supplemental Loans for Students (SLS) are made by a lender such as a bank, credit union, or savings and loan association.

SLS loans have variable interest rates, adjusted each year. The current rate is 12 percent. Under SLS, undergraduates and graduate students can borrow up to $4,000 a year, to a total of $20,000. This amount is in addition to the Stafford Loan limits. Unlike Stafford Loan borrowers, SLS borrowers do not have to show need; like all borrowers, however, they may have to undergo a credit analysis.

Before you can receive an SLS loan, your school must determine your eligibility for a Stafford Loan and a Pell Grant. If you're eligible for aid from either or both of those programs, this amount may affect the amount you can borrow under SLS. Under SLS, as with the Stafford Loan Program, you can't borrow more than the cost of your education.

SLS borrowers get the same deferments as Stafford Loan borrowers (check with your lending agency), except that under SLS the deferments apply only to loan principal. There is no grace period for SLS repayment.

State Assistance

Every state has a program of grants, scholarships, and loans for residents attending college in the state. Appendix D lists the addresses and phone numbers of each state office that deals with loans and award programs.

Aid from the School

In addition to administering campus-based federal aid programs, most schools have scholarship and loan monies of their own. Many match scholarships from other sources, some have installment plans, and over half give scholarships based on merit.

Alverno College in Milwaukee is typical in that it has a scholarship pool consisting of over seventy-five awards that are created from private foundations and are specifically for reentry women. Among them are:

- The Rita Barlow Memorial Scholarship, for a senior nursing student who is going into community health nursing.
- The Emil Blatz Memorial Scholarship, for Milwaukee-area students who meet Alverno's scholarship standards.
- The Alfred and Hilda Case Scholarship, for continuing education students who need financial assistance.
- The Gardner Scholarship, providing full tuition for a Hispanic woman.
- The P. H. Orth Company Scholarship, for working students attending Alverno's Weekend College.

For information about the awards offered by the school you're considering, check with its financial aid officer, who should be able to give you a list. Also check with the head of the department in which you plan to study. Some departments have their own scholarships or prizes. If you are a member of a minority group, contact the school's minority affairs office and ask for information on aid for minority students. The number of tuition scholarships for minority students is steadily increasing with the growth of corporate interest in minorities in the work force.

Private Scholarships

In addition to federal and state aid, millions of dollars in private scholarship money is awarded each year. Many programs do not even require that you show need. Appendix E gives a selected list of scholarships and other awards from such sources as governmental organizations, private professional organizations, foundations, and women's clubs.

Corporations

Some companies offer scholarships or tuition benefits to their employees or their employees' children. The Knogo Corporation of Hauppauge, New York, a manufacturer of antitheft devices, reimburses 100 percent of employees' tuition if they maintain at least a B average. The maximum amount Knogo will pay per student in any one year is $1,800. Maritz, Inc., in Fenton, Missouri, will pay 75 percent of tuition costs, with no maximum, as long as employees take 16 credits or less each year.

Some corporations also offer scholarships to specific groups of students; for example, those of Scandinavian descent, women over 25, or those living in a certain community. To find out the full range of what's available, contact the public relations departments of major companies headquartered in your area, as well as trade and professional associations connected with your field of study.

If you are already in college and have declared a major, ask your financial aid officer for help in locating money from companies in your field. The main branches of public libraries also have reference books listing corporations that award scholarship money to students.

Labor Unions

Many labor unions offer tuition benefits and scholarships to members and their families. In Appendix C, you will find a list by state of district, regional, and local union scholarships. For a list of national and international awards from the unions, write to the

AFL-CIO Department of Education, 815 16th Street, NW, Room 407, Washington, DC 20006, and ask for *The AFL-CIO Guide to Union Sponsored Scholarships, Awards, and Student Financial Aid.*

Community Groups

A variety of community groups make financial aid available to students. Call or write your local chamber of commerce. Contact the local YWCA, civic associations, social clubs, women's organizations, and women's committees or caucuses within professional associations. Ask for a list of financial aid sources.

The Military

For those interested in military training, the Army, Air Force, and Naval Reserve Officer Training Corps (ROTC) programs offer money for school in return for six years of military service, four of them on active duty. Ask local recruiters or the ROTC office on your intended campus for information about scholarships and other education assistance. If you are a veteran or the spouse or child of a deceased or disabled veteran, ask your Veterans Administration office whether you qualify for education benefits.

Chapter

6

Support Services

Colleges and universities have always provided a wide array of on-campus support services to assist their students. Today, however, as adults and particularly women increasingly make their presence known in classrooms and on campuses formerly devoted exclusively to 18- to 22-year-old students, the definition of "support services" is changing dramatically.

Almost every institution provides what are known as "the basic services": housing, dining halls, medical insurance, health-care programs, student employment and graduate placement services, legal services, and extracurricular activities. Some schools also offer special transportation services or facilities for commuting students. Most offer initiation workshops or distribute publications telling what services are available, as well as where and how to take advantage of them.

When a school is catering to an adult population, however, especially one that is largely female, such basic services are a long way from being adequate. As described so well in the following quote from Antioch University's brochure for its Center for Adult Learning, adult students are different.

> Adult students have special needs and capacities. Based on twenty years of experience in diverse cities, the Antioch faculty believes that the learning strategies and academic climate appropriate to working adults returning to school is significantly different from the strategies and climate adopted for 18-22 year-old undergraduates. Thus, Antioch's Center for Adult Learning has been designed with a specific set of assumptions in mind. We believe that most adults need:
>
> - Respect for their autonomy. Adults don't like traditional forms of education which patronize students of all ages. Grades and multiple choice tests should be used rarely. (The Antioch program uses narrative evaluations of course work both by faculty and students);

- Respect for their maturity while also understanding that some adults may be more set in their ways, and that they will need help managing the stress caused by the program. While working adults bring special strengths, they also bring special problems. They may need workshops in certain learning skills, in degree and career planning, and in stress management;
- Respect for a complex life based upon multiple roles. The school should be set up to accommodate adult students who possess a more complex worldview;
- Respect for the greater self-discipline which adults have developed. Adults can concentrate better and for longer periods of time than younger students. They don't appreciate large lecture classes, but they can handle long, intense seminars. They can also better manage independent projects;
- Respect for their greater self-understanding. Adults are more aware of their own limits and biases than younger students. Understanding the shortness of life, many adults are searching to improve their roles as providers and teachers. They can also immediately benefit (and help others to benefit) by studying themselves as both learners and teachers;
- Respect for the valuable experience that generally comes with age. Much real learning goes unrecognized by either the student or society in general. Compared to younger cohorts, adults have had years of experience in the world and, unlike most younger undergraduates, continue to have experiences at work and home as they enact multiple roles. They have learned a great deal even though many will not initially recognize or value the real knowledge they have acquired. . . .

Adult students are more likely than their classmates to be married or to have been married. They are more likely to have children. They tend to learn best in settings that maximize the importance of experiential learning.

Because they rarely live on campus, adult students may find it difficult to investigate student employment opportunities or to obtain affordable health care. Further, institutional policies and practices regarding campus employment, medical insurance, health care, and other basic services may inadvertently exclude or discriminate against adults, especially adult women.

This chapter will discuss a number of support services designed specifically for reentry women. If you are lucky enough to have a choice of schools, you may want to draw up a checklist of which offers what and use this to help you make your decision.

Child Care

A study conducted by the Office for Student Services at the University of Michigan found that a fifth to a quarter of the female students participating in the survey said that they positively would seek more employment or more education if child-care services were available.

While an increasing number of families share child care equally between mother and father, an overwhelming majority still believe that women, having been socialized as the primary child-rearers, should assume full responsibility. In the abstract, child care is not an issue confined solely to women; in reality, however, it is probably *the* number one issue for most women.

"I had two children under the age of 7 when I decided to go back to school," says Sheera Spencer, a 37-year-old student who will be graduating this spring with a degree in counseling. "My husband said he would help out with child care as much as he could, but what that turned out to mean was that he'd take the kids to Grandma's when I was at my wit's end studying for finals. His position was based on what he called 'our original deal' — he'd go to work, and I'd take care of the children."

Sheera made it through school by relying on a constantly changing network of child-care services, ranging from a neighborhood cooperative baby-sitting center to a series of public and private day-care facilities near the campus. "It has taken me six years to finish a degree that should have taken, at most, three," she says. "If I had it to do over, I'd definitely choose a school that had its own day-care services, even if it meant traveling three times as far to get there."

Despite the fact that nearly two thirds of reentry women have children under the age of 10, institutions continue to be slow in addressing the issue of how to provide child-care services. "You'd think," says a third-year student of physical education at Ohio State University who is the mother of twin 4-year-old boys, "that schools would realize what side their bread is buttered on.

"Most schools," she says, "would really be hurting if it wasn't for us — women coming back to finish their education. When are they going to say 'thank you' and help us out with what *we* need, namely on-campus child care?"

While many women feel that schools are dragging their feet on the issue of child care (to the point at which a number of women's organizations are considering class actions charging discrimination in terms of equal access to opportunities for employment training), others see increasing numbers of institutions commit-

79

ting themselves to some form of on-campus service. In fact, a study of postsecondary institutions conducted by the Women's Bureau of the Department of Labor turned up the following evidence showing that, if it's not an all-out effort, at least *something* is happening:

- One in every four campuses among the 1,100 four-year institutions surveyed had some kind of preschool program.
- Approximately 425 preschool programs existed on American campuses at the time of the study. About 90 were designated as day-care centers, 135 as nursery-school programs, 75 as laboratory-school programs, and 125 as combination types.
- Roughly 17,000 children attended some kind of preschool program on campus.
- About 32 percent of the programs charged fees. Those that did charged an average of $10 weekly per child.
- The vast majority of campus programs (three out of four) depended on nonuniversity funds for the bulk of their operating expenses, demonstrating that schools are willing to look elsewhere for the funding of things that they consider to be important.

Many states have turned campus day care into a political issue, postulating that the absence of campus day care discriminates against the full participation of women students. A large number of cities and states now mandate budgetary allotments to pay for child-care services on campus.

All twenty institutions of the City University of New York, for example—nine 4-year colleges, seven community colleges, a law school, a graduate school of arts and sciences, and an affiliated medical school—now have day-care centers supported by a combination of city and state funds. The University of Connecticut System, where 66 percent of the 36,000 undergraduates are 25 and older and nearly half the undergraduates and graduate students attend part-time, has also made day care a campus feature.

Some schools, while not yet actually providing day care, have gone the route of offering special services for women with children. Mills College in Oakland, California, for example, where adults represent more than a fifth of the college's 1,056 students, recently recategorized twenty-four apartments previously reserved for juniors and seniors as specifically for adult students with children. The University of California, Santa Cruz, where 1,500 of the 9,000 students are over 25, provides subsidized family housing.

If child care is an issue for you in determining either whether you *can* go back to school or how many courses you can take, you should consult with a school adviser about whether any of the following options are available:

- **Family day care.** Some schools contract with fully licensed, state-approved family day-care centers to provide space for a certain number of postsecondary students' children in exchange for institutional contributions to subsidize these centers.
- **On-campus preschools or nursery schools.** Find out whether such schools operate on a full- or half-day basis and whether you will be given priority consideration for course scheduling around those hours.
- **College-subsidized day-care centers.** These may be run by public agencies, by parent cooperatives, or by for-profit or not-for-profit organizations. They will be located near the school and subsidized entirely or in part by the school.
- **Laboratory schools.** These are designed primarily for teacher-training programs, but they also provide care for the children of students. Although parents usually pay to enroll their children in such schools, parents who are students are charged a reduced rate, particularly if they are majoring in an area related to child development.
- **Drop-off centers, baby-sitting services, or playrooms.** Many institutions have now begun offering such short-term on-campus services for women taking only one or two courses. Some of these services require advance reservations, while others take children as their parents' need arises.
- **Cooperative day-care centers.** These have increased in number on campus, as well as in many communities. At some colleges and universities, cooperatives are run by student parents, who share the responsibility of providing care for their children. Professional staff are usually hired by the cooperative, whose members may assist in teaching, providing and maintaining equipment, and so on. These centers may be in a convenient location, such as a family housing facility, and they generally operate with minimal funds. The quality of care depends in part upon the commitment of the cooperative's members.
- **Combination programs.** These programs, although unusual, are perhaps the most comprehensive form of child-care service available, because they provide a wide range of

services to meet the varying needs of students. California's De Anza College, for example, has a child development center that combines training programs for adults with a variety of programs for preschool children. The center operates four distinct programs: an enrichment class for 2-year-olds; a state-funded, full-day preschool; a parent cooperative; and an early childhood development laboratory training school. The first three programs serve the children of student parents, while the last serves children of the community at the same time that it trains college students interested in careers in early childhood education.

Make sure, when you investigate all the available options, that you have a clear picture in mind of how a well-run child-care center should look. In painting that picture, you might want to keep in mind the following questions:

- Is the facility clean?
- Do most of the children seem happy, or are a number of them crying? All children cry sometimes, but you should be able to distinguish between "normal" crying and crying that signals neglect.
- Do the people in charge seem to like the children, or are they bored, annoyed, and tired?
- What's the ratio of adults to children? Most people are comfortable with a 1:5 ratio for infants and toddlers, and a 1:10 ratio for young children.
- Is the program geared mainly toward passing time till parents show up to take their children home, or is there some goal related to education or socialization? In most cases, you will want to make sure that your child-care provider is contributing to your child's development, not just providing for his or her bodily care.
- What kind of food is served? Is it in keeping with what you think your child should be eating? Would you feel comfortable making your dietary desires known?
- Were you made to feel welcome, or did you sense nervousness, resentment, or even hostility? Trust your gut feeling on this one.

There are a number of publications to help ease the process of choosing a child-care provider. Some of the best are *Day Care—A Parent's Choice* by James and Julie Hollingsworth (D/B Publishing Trust, New York), *Child Care That Works* by Ann Muscari and Wenda Wardell Morrone (Doubleday, New York), and *The Parent/*

Child Manual on Daycare by Charlene Solomon (Tom Doherty Associates, New York).

Counseling Services

"My first semester back in school I gained 12 pounds," says Carolyn Warrick, a sophomore in a health administration program. "I felt insecure about whether or not I could do the work, especially when I realized that I hadn't written a paper or read a textbook in twenty years. In addition, I was constantly forgetting when I had assignments due and where I'd put the notes I'd taken in a certain class. I had no idea how to set up a schedule, no idea how to do research, and absolutely no conception of what it meant to be a student while trying to maintain a relationship with my husband and children.

"The worst part was that I thought I could figure it all out myself without asking anybody for help. One day, at the end of my rope, I went over to the counseling center to see what they offered. After one session, they had steered me into a series of prep courses in math and study skills and assigned me a personal counselor to help arrange my schedule. If it hadn't been for them, I might have eaten myself into oblivion."

Like all groups of students, women going back to school have their own set of problems and concerns. For some, it's worrying about the papers they know they'll have to write; for others, it's a sense that they don't belong, that they're outsiders.

Most studies show that whether they are 66 or 26, whether they've had some college experience or none, and whether they were good or poor students in high school, the basic difficulties encountered by reentry women usually fall into one or more of the following categories:

- Problems with the academic process, including policies and procedures with respect to applications, admission, enrollment, transfer of credit, and scheduling.
- Problems with the situation, including such things as children in need of day care, transportation difficulties, and financial limitations.
- Problems with personal concerns, including a general lack of confidence about skills and abilities, academic insecurity, an unsupportive family or spouse, and feelings of guilt.

Most colleges have three kinds of counseling services available to handle the above problems: academic, personal, and career or vocational. Sometimes the three overlap, and the end of one may be indistinguishable from the beginning of another. Sometimes all three are sponsored by the college counseling center itself; sometimes they are put together by groups of students with the center's permission.

When you're finding out what kinds of counseling services are available, you should be aware that they can take any of the following forms:

- Traditional individual counseling.
- Individual peer counseling.
- Group counseling.
- Support groups, facilitated by peers or professionals.
- Rap groups.
- Assertiveness training.
- Values clarification.
- Brown-bag lunch groups.
- Special interest groups, such as divorced women's groups, displaced homemakers' groups, or groups for mothers of preschool children.
- Credit or noncredit courses focusing on specific subjects, such as career guidance, math avoidance, study skills, and job preparation.
- Weekend seminars.
- Preadmission programs designed to aid a woman in deciding whether or not to return to school.
- Parenting courses for those who use child-care services on campus or for reentry parents in general.

Counseling services can also be provided formally or informally in a variety of settings throughout the institution. Some possible locations are:

- Continuing education or reentry program offices.
- Women's centers.
- Counseling centers.
- Administrative offices.
- Deans' offices.
- Admissions offices.
- Career planning offices.
- Academic departments.
- Financial aid offices.
- Minority affairs offices or centers.
- Health centers.

When women who have used on-campus counseling services talk about why they decided to go, their reasons have to do not with needing therapy but with needing support. The following are typical of statements made by some of these women:

> "I needed encouragement from people who had gone back . . . to hear that it wasn't strange for someone my age to be on campus."

> "The thing I needed most was to know that there were other women in my situation, women who felt like chickens without heads from morning till night because they were balancing so many roles."

> "My main problem in going back to school was that I had no idea how to negotiate my way through such a gigantic university bureaucracy."

> "Before I started school, I had dreams about how everybody in my class would know what was going on except me. I needed reassurance that I also had something to contribute, that I wasn't going to stand out like some old dumbbell."

According to college counselors, problems encountered by reentry women usually stem from one of the following situations. First, they've always been dependent on others for their sense of self; they've moved from dependency on the family as a child to a similar dependency on a husband or family as an adult. Now they've decided to go back to school, and the reentry process becomes a time of new awareness of themselves as having an independent identity. In order to be able to get along academically and personally, such women find they have to make decisions and act independently of any other person. For most, this is extremely frightening.

Second, as women engage in activities outside the home, they feel an urgent need for personal success and achievement. They want everything to be done *now* and perfectly, and they become extremely competitive, feeling that they have to prove themselves. Anything short of an A or a 4.0 average will not do. They sometimes drive themselves too hard and are unrelenting in their quest for goal attainment.

The longer a woman has been out of school, the greater her fears are likely to be with respect to going back. These may include fear of dulled skills and intellectual abilities, fear of coping with

85

added pressures and responsibilities, guilt concerning the financial expenditure for her education, and guilt over time spent away from her family.

Societal prejudices with respect to age may make an older woman feel physically, socially, and psychologically out of place on campus, especially if she is enrolled in a program where most of the students are traditionally younger men. This may lead to a heightened sense of aging and a general sense of worthlessness.

Reentry women sometimes feel an initial sense of loss when they go back to school. This consists of feelings of loss of community and personal networks, loss of ongoing contact with spouse and children, and loss of economic status (if they are going back to school full-time after having worked and earned a good salary).

Basic Skills Counseling

A significant number of reentry women from all backgrounds may lack confidence in their academic abilities initially and feel that they need remedial help in language, math, or science skills. Different schools handle basic skills education in different ways. Some have found ways to work cooperatively with community organizations to provide basic skills training. Some have set up special remedial departments, complete with separate faculty members and separate sources of funding. The women's program at San Jose City College in California, for example, offers a one-semester college preparation program designed for women whose primary language is not English. The noncredit course is open to any woman who wants training in basic English before beginning regular college classes.

The majority of schools, however, provide basic skills training and remedial courses as part of their general offerings. At De Anza College, students are tested not only to determine academic achievement levels but also to see how they learn best (visually, aurally, etc.). Individual programs, taken for credit, are designed for those with particular learning needs.

Miami-Dade Community College, which serves 70,000 students, more than half of them born outside the United States, uses an "academic alert" system. Midway through the semester, students receive a letter summarizing their progress in each course and directing them to college centers or individuals for assistance if their work falls below a certain grade level.

At New York University, reentry students can choose to undergo a series of "placement tests" to see whether they will be able to handle college-level material. If the results indicate a need, they can take a series of credit-granting courses to sharpen their basic skills. Titles include Study Strategies for College, Math Strategies for College, and Writing Strategies for College.

Personal Counseling

As with any situation involving change, development, and transition, the initial reentry process may be a time of "identity crisis." You probably will go through a period of self-evaluation, discovery, and personal growth. You will experience many moments when you feel "high" about what you are attempting to do; however, you also may experience an equal number of moments when you feel painful self-doubt and anxiety.

Seeking out the counseling services at your school can help you deal with these feelings as you search for new meaning in your life. In most cases, you will be served best by programs developed specifically to deal with the concerns of returning women (women's continuing education programs, women's centers, reentry programs, etc.).

The Adult Life Resource Center at the University of Kansas, for example, offers a workshop focusing on the changes and problems associated with various stages in women's adult development and strategies for dealing with them. In the District of Columbia, George Washington University's Continuing Education for Women Center uses former or upperclass reentry women as an integral part of their group counseling program. Each woman in the program is assigned an adult version of a "big sister" to help her sift through the hundreds of different feelings—some of them negative—associated with going back to school.

Many schools also have counseling services for special populations. Miami-Dade Community College in Florida offers bilingual group counseling to displaced homemakers. Blackfeet Community College in Browning, Montana, has a counseling center for Native American women who are single heads of households, working women, or older women. The center provides financial aid and child-care services, as well as counseling for nontraditional careers. Old Dominion University in Virginia offers a course titled Black Women and Identity to explore the historical background of the topic and help black women develop strategies for strengthening their sense of self.

Career or Vocational Counseling

In addition to skills counseling and personal counseling, you should also check into what is offered by your school's vocational counseling center. Such centers can provide you with information on career choices, help you deal with any feelings of self-doubt with respect to getting a job, and show you how to go about seeking and applying for employment.

Many schools now have services that include computerized links to databases maintained by state and federal departments of industry and labor, allowing users to track current job trends. Some have mandatory internships at intervals during the educational program so that students can combine their theoretical education with a practical, hands-on one.

Milwaukee's Alverno College has been singled out by college presidents in recent national surveys for its efforts in reaching out to adult women. It offers the Alverno Contact System, which puts students in touch with a network of over 1,500 alumnae and 2,000 community professionals who have volunteered to serve as personal career resources. In addition, the career lab offers self-scoring career-assessment inventories and information files on hundreds of companies and agencies nationwide.

Information Services

Ideally, the school you have chosen has a handbook listing and describing the services it makes available to adult women returning to school. It should include the hours of operation for these services and the name and phone number of a person or office that can be contacted for additional information about each entry in the handbook.

If you're lucky, your school's information services will operate on a schedule that includes extended hours for administrative offices, counseling centers, advisory personnel, and so on. Many schools lack the resources to keep extended hours on a daily basis and compensate for this by keeping offices open later one or two nights a week and for a few hours on the weekend. Maryland's Hood College, for example, keeps its library, health center, and learning assessment and resource center open regularly in the evenings, while its admissions office, continuing education office, financial aid office, and registrar's office are kept open one night a week, as are its student affairs department and its student bank.

Another helpful feature you may find listed in your booklet of services is a special department keeping the academic records of adult students. Such departments increasingly are being set up in response to adult students' complaints about the inaccessibility to them of registrars' offices that are open only during conventional business hours. At Chicago's Saint Xavier College, duplicate records, transcripts, grade reports, and the like are kept in the department of continuing education's administrative unit. This office has evening and weekend hours and is responsible for the records of all adult students, whether they attend days, evenings, or weekends. In this way, students who need registration assistance or information on how to initiate the procedure for challenging a course grade have an opportunity to discuss solutions to their problems at a time that suits *their* schedule instead of the school's.

Transportation and Commuter Services

Transportation to, from, and around campus is a critical need for many reentry women, who are more likely to commute to school than to live on campus. Returning women tend to enroll for classes at nontraditional times, usually at night. Many are discouraged by a fear of commuting after a certain hour. Some schools have agreements with community bus lines to offer special fares or special routings to accommodate evening students. At Edmonds Community College in Washington, reentry students indicated their preference for public over private transportation in getting to and from campus. The school responded by working out an agreement with the city, by which the municipal bus system makes regularly scheduled stops at the college's senior center.

In Iowa, Simpson College offered students a tuition reimbursement based on how far they traveled to the campus and the number of trips they made in an average week. Their slogan was: "You take the class. We'll pay the gas."

Georgetown University operates five minibus routes in the greater Washington, D.C., area and provides services for students traveling from off-campus housing to the main campus and the law center. Buses are operated by students employed part-time and carry passengers with student ID's for a fare of 50 cents.

A few colleges have purchased their own minibuses or jitneys to accommodate students in outlying areas. The University of Nevada–Reno, for example, coordinates the use of its own jitneys with the use of city buses to provide transportation for people who live within a 20-mile radius of Reno and need a free ride to the campus.

Medical Insurance and Health-Care Services

How students pay for medical insurance and health-care services varies from campus to campus. Upon enrollment, students often pay a mandatory comprehensive fee to cover general college expenses. This single fee typically covers the cost of medical insurance, use of the campus infirmary, and some related medical expenses. At other schools, students may pay a separate fee for medical insurance and/or health-care services on either a mandatory or an elective basis.

Whatever form of insurance and health care is available, it is often extended to full-time students only. Because part-time or nontraditional students may not be eligible, reentry women often find themselves without affordable coverage, unless they are employed and already participating in a group plan or unless they are covered by a spouse's plan.

Reentry women may also find that some insurance companies have policies that, in effect, discriminate against them. In some states, reduced rates on student health insurance policies are available only to students between the ages of 19 and 26.

Before you assume that you automatically will be covered under a school's insurance policy or that you automatically will be eligible to take advantage of student health-care services, find out whether there are a certain number of courses you need to take to be covered, how much such coverage costs, and whether there is an age limit for inclusion. Some schools offer students the opportunity to purchase family medical insurance; ask if your school participates in such a plan. Find out the hours of operation of the student health services.

You should also find out whether your school makes any provision for contacting you should a family emergency occur. At Northwestern University in Illinois, female students can leave the telephone number of the women's programs office with their child-care providers, their children's schools, and their husband's employer. They also supply the office with a copy of their own schedules, so that if anything happens, the office has a set procedure for notifying the student immediately. The University of Maryland College Park operates a similar service.

Chapter

7

Sexual Harassment

Janice Maccoby is one of the few women in her class at engineering school. Initially, she was very enthusiastic about going back for her degree after having raised three children, but now she feels she may not finish. The problem is that many of her professors continually refer to female engineering students and engineers in such lewd and belittling ways that Janice is rethinking whether it's the field she wants to enter. She has considered discussing her feelings with a member of the administration but doubts that she would be given a fair hearing.

Linda DeLillo is in her last year of an undergraduate program in psychology, and until now her grade point average has been 3.5 or better. This term she is taking a class in family counseling with a professor who is well-known for "getting involved" with his students. He repeatedly has asked her for a date, a proposition she has always refused. Now, as the class approaches the midterm, he tells her that her work is under par and that she will have to do a number of extra papers if she hopes to pass. Linda is sure that he is retaliating for her refusal to go out with him. She considers going to the head of the department but is afraid she might be singled out as a troublemaker.

Karen Gershowitz is a work-study student in the registrar's office. She depends on her income from the job to help pay her graduate school tuition and would have a hard time continuing in the program without it. One day, after everybody has gone home, she is alone in the back office with her boss, a divorced man in his forties. He puts his arm around her shoulder and invites her to come home with him that evening. Karen refuses and continues to refuse all the next week, as his overtures persist. She wants to report his behavior but is afraid she will lose her job.

Sexual harassment is defined as any unwelcome, offensive sexual behavior, either physical or verbal, that embarrasses, humiliates, or intimidates. It is a type of behavior whose focal point is power, not sex; harassers use their positions of power or authority to overstep the boundaries between the professional and the personal. They introduce a sexual element into what should be a sex-neutral situation, and they do it despite—or, in some cases, because of—a lack of reciprocation.

The difference between voluntary sexual relationships and sexual harassment is that harassment contains elements of coercion, threat, and unwanted attention that can be present either from the very beginning or after a certain amount of time during which there even may have been a reciprocal interest.

As the issue of harassment has continued to gain widespread publicity (especially with the higher-than-average number of date rapes reported on college campuses recently), a few nationally prominent male academics have set themselves up as peacemakers, dismissing the charges of harassment with sarcastic comments about the number of times they themselves have been propositioned. They have been quoted in national newspapers and magazines as asking, what about female students who "come on" to them for entire semesters with absolutely no reciprocation on their part?

The difference is that these "spokesmen" always have the power to say "no" without fear of losing a grade or a job. Normally, a person can exercise freedom of choice about whether she wishes to establish an intimate relationship with someone without fear of the consequences. This element is missing in cases of sexual harassment, where one party holds a position of power over the other.

"Last semester I had to take statistics," says a second-year graduate student in psychology. "I struggled through the entire term and, by the time final exams rolled around, I knew I needed at least a B to pass the course. On exam day, I was sitting in the back of the room, feeling like there was no way I was going to make it, when my professor came up to me. All semester he'd been eyeing me, and I had taken to sitting way in the back of the room and leaving through the side door. When I lifted my head to see what he wanted, I saw him looking down my blouse and smiling in a sinister way.

"'Don't worry about your grade,' he said. 'I'll give your exam my special attention. You can pick it up this afternoon after 4.' Well, I never went to his office, and I wound up getting a B. But to this day, I blame myself for letting him get away with that kind of harassment. He knew I needed to pass that course, and he used it against me, figuring I wouldn't rock the boat."

Twenty-five to 35 percent of all female college students experience some form of sexual harassment, ranging from sexist comments to direct solicitations for sexual favors to assault. Five percent, or 150,000 women a year, experience direct threats or the offer of bribes for sexual favors. A few schools have specific policies banning some or all forms of sexual harassment. Most do not.

While all women are targets for harassment, four groups stand out as being considerably more vulnerable than others:

1. Women who enter nontraditional fields of study. These women may become the target of sexist comments and treatment because of a perception that they will be "taking a job away from a man who *really* needs it," or because they are "barging into an area where women don't belong."
2. Reentry women who are closer in age to their instructors and who, because of their enthusiasm, tend to involve themselves in closer working relationships with professors. Such enthusiasm is often misinterpreted as indicative of sexual interest.
3. Minority women who may be harassed sexually as a form of racial stereotyping (e.g., black women are more "sexually available," Latin women are "hot").
4. Young, shy, or inexperienced women whose unassertive manner is interpreted by particularly power-hungry harassers as a signal that this person is "easy to exploit."

Misconceptions

Despite both an increase in the reporting of cases of harassment and a general growth in public awareness of the nature of harassment, a number of misconceptions still exist. The following looks at some of the most common misconceptions.

Myths About Sexual Harassment

MYTH: Sexual harassment only happens to women who are provocatively dressed.

FACT: Sexual harassment can happen to anyone, no matter how she dresses.

MYTH: If the woman had only said "NO" to the harasser, he would have stopped immediately.
FACT: Many harassers are told "NO" repeatedly and it does no good. NO is too often heard as YES.

MYTH: If a woman ignores sexual harassment, it will go away.
FACT: No, it won't. Generally, the harasser is a repeat offender who will not stop on his own. Ignoring it may be seen as assent or encouragement.

MYTH: All men are harassers.
FACT: No, only a few men harass. Usually there is a pattern of harassment: one man harasses a number of women either sequentially or simultaneously, or both.

MYTH: Sexual harassment is harmless. Women who object have no sense of humor.
FACT: Harassment is humiliating and degrading. It undermines school careers and often threatens economic livelihood. No one should have to endure humiliation with a smile.

MYTH: Sexual harassment affects only a few people.
FACT: Surveys on campus show that up to 30 percent of all female college students experience some form of sexual harassment. Some surveys of women in the working world have shown that as many as 70 percent have been sexually harassed in some way.

Source: Association of American Colleges, Project on the Status and Education of Women, April 1986.

Forms of Sexual Harassment

When you are confronted with what you suspect may be sexual harassment, it is important to remember that what is humiliating or intimidating to you may not have the same effect on somebody else. This is not to say that you are not experiencing harassment or that some other person is more tolerant than you. It's just that some forms of harassment are universally acknowledged as such, and others are more dependent on individual sensitivity.

Most sexual harassment falls into one of two categories: verbal or physical. Examples of verbal harassment may include the following:

- Sexual innuendos or remarks about your clothing, body, or sexual activities. ("Great nipples." "So you're studying to be a therapist. I'll lie on the couch for you anytime." "What did you *do* to get that grade? Sleep with him?")
- Suggestive or insulting sounds, including "wolf whistles."
- Jokes about sex or women that have as their intent the denigration of women.
- Sexual propositions, invitations, or other pressures for sex. ("Most of the books I have on this subject are at home. Why don't you come over tonight around 9, and that way we'll get to know each other better in a more private setting?")
- Implied or overt threats. ("You want an A, you know what to do.")

Physical harassment may include:

- Patting, pinching, and other touching that is inappropriate and unwanted, especially if the offender already has been told that it is unwanted.
- Brushing against the body when this could easily be avoided.
- Attempted or actual kissing or fondling when this is clearly unwanted and unsolicited.
- Forcible sexual assault, including cases where the woman initially may have entered into a situation of intimacy voluntarily. Regardless of what anybody says to the contrary (and there is a great deal of controversy surrounding situations that women enter voluntarily), it is a woman's right to say "no" at any time and expect that it be honored.
- Leering or ogling (for example, staring at a student's breasts or openly looking her up and down when she walks across the room).
- Making obscene gestures that have as their main purpose humiliation.

What You Can Do

There are a number of tried-and-true strategies for defusing situations involving harassment. First, however, let's take a look at a list of things which you should *never* do under any circumstances.

You should never blame yourself. You did not cause this to happen, no matter what your relationship to the man was prior to the offending incident. Whatever your actions preceding the harassment, it is the harasser who decided to engage in his action. He and only he is responsible for his behavior. Blaming yourself only sets you up as a victim, which further plays into the hands of the offender. By blaming yourself, you are turning your anger inward, which is the first step to depression. What you need to do is turn your anger *outward,* toward him!

You should never delay action in the hope that the harasser will stop. Maybe he will. But if he doesn't, you've lost time and maybe led him to believe that what he's doing is all right with you. Also, if it should come eventually to a point where you wish to file charges, any delay on your part may cause you to exceed the time limit for doing so.

Never keep the harassment to yourself. First of all, you're missing a great opportunity to warn others who may be affected by the same harasser. Also, you are denying yourself the support of people who may have gone through the same thing or may know somebody who has. You did nothing wrong. There's no reason to hide the fact that you're being harassed. It's when you talk about your fear and humiliation that you gain power over them. Being silent—and therefore alone—only makes you feel more like a victim.

Now, on to a list of informal strategies that have as their main goal conciliation rather than punishment. First, you should know your rights. Sexual harassment is illegal in many instances, but not in all. Ask your adviser or the dean of student affairs for an explanation of your particular school's policy regarding the different types of harassment.

Speak up at the time. Say "no" immediately, firmly, clearly, and with absolutely no smile on your face. This is not a time to be polite or to sublimate your feelings under a cover of concern for the offender's sensitivities. Don't apologize for feeling the way you're feeling. Don't, for example, say, "I know you're going to think I'm being a prude, but . . ." Don't make anyone else the reason for your objection. ("My boyfriend wouldn't like it if I went out on a date.") Such statements only encourage the determined harasser to believe that you might respond differently if he removes or gets around the obstacle.

Keep a journal or other record of dates, places, times, witnesses, and the nature of the harassment. State clearly what the person did and how you responded. Keep any letters or notes received. Keep a list of whom you contacted to complain about the harassment and of what was done.

Tell someone, such as another student or a coworker. Find out if others have been harassed by the same person and if anybody will support you should you decide to take action. Rarely do harassers engage in their offensive behavior one time only; usually it's part of a long-term pattern that can be traced and documented.

Find an advocate, perhaps a counselor, perhaps a mentor (see Chapter 8), who can give you emotional support as well as information about institutional policies and people to contact.

Many people have successfully stopped sexual harassment by writing a special kind of letter to the harasser. Your letter should be polite, formal, low-key, and detailed, and it should consist of three parts:

1. A factual account of what happened, without any evaluation of the incident or emotional comment. You should not, for example, include in this part how upset you were by the harassing behavior or threaten any long-term action. You should not attempt to reform the harasser or find reasons to explain his behavior. Stick to a reporting kind of format: "Last week, when I came to your office to discuss my paper, you looked at my breasts, patted my knee, and made a number of comments about my body."
2. A description of how you felt about the event, without assigning blame. Not "You made me feel humiliated," but "I felt humiliated." Not "Your actions have made me consider dropping out of the program," but "I have considered leaving the program." Do not in any way apologize for your feelings.
3. A plan for what you want to happen next. Since this is your first attempt at stopping the behavior, you want to avoid bringing in other resources and simply ask that the offender discontinue the offensive behavior. "I don't ever want you to touch me or make reference to my body again," or "I want you to retract your statements about failing me and grade me according to my work." Again, make no threats or assignment of blame. Also, show no hesitancy in stating your plan. Don't say, "I know this is going to sound like I'm creating a mountain out of a molehill, but I would appreciate it if you would refrain from making remarks about my appearance."

This letter should be sent by certified or registered mail, and you should keep a copy. At this point, you are trying to settle the situation between the two of you; you are not yet sending copies to administrators. In most cases, the harasser will stop, either because he was shocked to his senses when he heard your description of his behavior (sometimes harassers come from environments where such statements or actions are interpreted as flattering and are not aware that all women don't see it that way) or because he fears that you will take your complaints to a higher level.

There are many advantages to writing this kind of letter. For one thing, since it's a form of communication that closes off the possibility of instantaneous feedback, it helps you regain a feeling of being in control. In a sense, you are having both the first and last word. Because of its confidentiality, it probably also will minimize or prevent retaliation. He may feel secure in the fact that you are choosing to settle the matter between the two of you and be grateful that you have not gone to the administration.

In addition, a personal letter addresses the unlikely but not impossible "what if" aspect of the situation: what if he's not even aware of the effects of his behavior? For example, in a department where men outnumber women ten to one, what if he is so unused to dealing with female students that he thinks his remarks were complimentary? Your choosing to deal with him on a one-to-one basis allows him to change his behavior, because he's been confronted with your humanity and your honest and no-fault account of how you felt rather than with the possibility of third-party punishment.

Studies have shown that personal letters more often than not stop the harassing behavior dead in its tracks. Look at it this way: at worst, you'll have to take the same next step you would have taken in the first place. You've lost nothing by trying.

What if the Harassment Doesn't Stop?

In a few very rare cases, you may need to go beyond the informal strategies suggested above or—as in cases where you fear the consequences of making your identity known—take a different route altogether.

If confidentiality is an issue, one of your options is to go to the chairperson of the relevant department and ask him or her to have a talk with the harasser. Present your story in terms of the facts: what happened, where, how many times, who else was present, etc. Your emphasis should be on reporting the situation, not on receiving counseling for your emotional distress. Also, remember that at this point you're simply asking for an end to the behavior, not for the imposition of sanctions.

Another method, not as effective but sometimes useful if you don't want to risk your name coming up in a personal talk between colleagues, is to ask the department chairperson to send a letter to the harasser himself or to all members of the department, reminding them of the institution's policies against sexual harassment. You may, however, find the head of the department unsympathetic to your request for personal reasons. Keep a record of your talk and consult someone else, possibly the dean of academic affairs.

If and when you have exhausted all possible informal routes, you may find you have no choice but to instigate more formal charges. Before doing anything, make sure you know the answers to the following questions:

- Has anyone used the formal grievance procedure before? If so, what happened?
- Who will conduct the eventual investigation?
- Who can help you prepare your case?
- Do you need an attorney?
- Can you bring an attorney or other person to the hearing?
- Will you be notified if the harasser decides to bring an attorney?
- If he brings an attorney, will you be cross-examined?
- Will your attorney be allowed to cross-examine the harasser?
- What is the time frame involved?
- What are the possible sanctions? (Possibilities include the harasser's being required to make a formal apology, being fined, being suspended, or being fired.)
- How much will this cost?
- Who will know that you have asked for this investigation?

While formal grievance procedures vary from school to school, they generally consist of the following steps. You or someone acting at your behest files a complaint. This usually involves a written description of what took place. A hearing is then scheduled to determine if the harassment occurred, how severe it was, and whether sanctions are warranted. Such hearings could be held in front of one person or before a committee of faculty members. Then a decision is made concerning what actions, if any, will be taken. If either you or the harasser is unhappy with the decision, an appeal can be filed.

When you go the route of formally charging somebody with harassment, you will need to have evidence to back up your claim. For good reason, your word against another's is rarely enough to win a case. This would be the time to show copies of a letter you wrote to the harasser, diary entries detailing the incident, or testimonials from witnesses or from others who have been harassed by the same person. The most important piece of evidence you can produce is one showing that you asked him to stop—once or repeatedly.

Never institute formal proceedings without at least some evidence of this sort. For one thing, you'll probably lose the case if you don't have evidence; for another, formal charges usually ruin careers, whether the person is found guilty or innocent. You should at least try to resolve the incident in a way that does a minimal amount of damage before reaching out to ruin him. While everybody at times acts from feelings of anger, hatred, or revenge, it is almost universally acknowledged that acting on such motivation only provokes the same kind of behavior back, but next time usually escalated by a few degrees.

Sexual Harassment and the Law

Sexual harassment is illegal in many but, sadly, not all cases. If, after exhausting more personal and informal strategies, you decide to take legal action, keep in mind that what laws exist are very specific. All lay the burden of proof on you, and obviously some types of proof are worth more than others. If you have a copy of a letter you sent to the harasser asking him to stop, after which the behavior continued, you will most likely win your case. If all you have, however, is an entry in your journal that talks about how awful it felt the day he tried to touch you, you can expect to be involved in a very shaky case.

The following sections describe the existing laws concerning sexual harassment.

Title IX

Since 1972, Title IX has prohibited sexual harassment of students in any part of any institution of higher education that receives federal funds. In 1984, however, the law was altered considerably: sexual harassment, a form of sexual discrimination, is now prohibited only in those *parts* or *programs* within an institution that receive federal funds. In other words, if only the office of minority assistance receives federal aid, then sexual harassment is prohibited only in that office and in classes run by that office.

For more information on Title IX, contact the Office for Civil Rights, U.S. Department of Education, Mary Switzer Building, 330 C Street, SW, Washington, DC 20202.

Title VII of the Civil Rights Act of 1964

According to the guidelines on sexual harassment under Title VII that were issued in 1980 by the Equal Employment Opportunity Commission, sexual harassment of employees is prohibited. This applies to students who are harassed when working either on campus or off campus, whether or not they are hired by the school.

For more information on Title VII, contact the Equal Employment Opportunity Commission, 2401 E Street, NW, Washington, DC 20507.

State Laws

Some states have laws against sexual harassment. To find out the law in your state, contact the following offices, most of which will be located in the state capital:

- The state civil rights commission.
- The state women's commission.
- The state fair employment practices commission, which deals with employment discrimination.
- The local office for civil rights (under the department of education).
- The local chapter of the National Organization for Women or any other women's group in your state or city.
- The local chapter of the American Civil Liberties Union.
- The state bar association, which might be able to refer you to appropriate sources of help.

To Date or Not to Date?

Finally, as a word of caution, *never* date your professor. To do so invites problems not only with him but also with other students, who will see signs of favoritism in his comments to you in class and in your grades.

Here's how the Association of American Colleges' Project on the Status and Education of Women put it in their report of April 1986:

What About Dating Your Professor?

The best time to date your professor, if at all, is *after* you have graduated from school. While it is true that some students have been able to date their professors without any problems, this is the exception rather than the rule. Some of the problems inherent in dating your professor are:

- When he has so much power over your grade(s) (and hence your future), it is difficult to have a relationship of equals;
- If your relationship is known to other people and your grades are excellent, some students and faculty may question the validity of your grades and find it hard to take you seriously as a student;
- If your relationship is secret, people could still find out about it and again question the validity of your grades. Because you have a personal relationship which is likely to influence your professor's objectivity, you yourself may be unsure of your true academic performance, which can lead to self-doubt;
- If the relationship ends badly with a lot of hard feelings on both sides, depending on his position,
  - he could sabotage your grade, or at least leave you wondering if his personal feelings influenced the grade;
  - he could talk about you to other teachers and negatively influence how they perceive you;
  - if he is the only one teaching any courses that you must take, it will be very awkward being in those classes. It will be difficult to ensure that his personal feelings wouldn't affect his behavior toward you in class or at grading time;
  - if he teaches in your major department, you might feel very uncomfortable not only with him but with others in the department as well. Indeed, some women go out of their way to avoid both a professor who is an ex-boyfriend and his department in general, and end up feeling alienated by the whole experience;
  - it would be extremely difficult to use him as a reference for graduate school or for employment. . . .

Chapter

8

Mentoring: A New Look at an Old Way to Get Ahead

Twenty years ago, the major problem for reentry women was a feeling of being outside of the academic process; their numbers were small, the amount of financial aid available to them was almost nonexistent, and there were virtually no support services geared toward their special needs. Today, however, with women the new student majority, the major problem is no longer finding a way to get inside the educational process but learning to *use* it in the best way possible for future career advancement.

One of the biggest stumbling blocks to that advancement, according to a number of recent studies, is that while in school women are less likely than men to identify the academic resources leading to career success. They generally don't advance as far or as fast as their male peers, and they have a tendency to stay within the boundaries of programs known for their "service" orientation. Also, because they are less confident about their chances for achievement than men, these women almost always avoid applying for programs that are known for academic excellence.

"Women, like most other people, tend to choose what's easy," says therapist Robin Scher. "It just so happens that what's easy for them is teaching, or counseling, or nursing. They *know* how to negotiate their way through those programs. They *know* they have the skills to be successful in those careers. If they were to choose engineering, where both the pay and the chances for advancement are much better, they'd have to struggle, initially through the math and science requirements and then in a field that's mostly male dominated. 'Why bother?' is what most women wind up telling themselves. If they had some help, some encouragement, someone telling them, 'you can do it' or 'I'm here to help,' things might be different."

Much anecdotal evidence and a number of recent studies have suggested that in school, as in the world of work, success depends not only on *what* you know but on *whom* you know; not only on hard work but also on the encouragement, guidance, support, and advocacy of already established people. These people can offer advice and constructive criticism and provide an overview of the system. They can warn you about political pitfalls and give you information about a variety of professional opportunities, as well as a ticket of admission.

Such people, usually referred to as "sponsors" or "mentors" (after the loyal and wise Mentor, a friend whom the Greek hero Odysseus entrusted with the education of his son), increasingly have been seen as crucial to professional development in general. The help they provide—in terms of the opportunities they bring to a relationship and the examples of behavior they set—can be especially important to women's success in academia.

Educators, like other professionals, operate primarily through what are known as "old-boy networks," in which standards for professional behavior and criteria for evaluating what's good and what isn't tend to be handed down from one generation to the next and communicated informally from one "old boy" to another. Interrelated networks of senior instructors not only determine in an informal way what issues are considered important but also often control access to academic awards, grant money, and potential job situations, largely on the strength of their own reputation and shared contacts. Those who are already established tend to act as "gatekeepers," restricting admission to those who are sponsored by another member of the system. Women students, because of their relative "newcomer" status, usually don't have this kind of sponsorship and are most often shut out.

As one professor explains, "When it comes to higher education, men make the rules. Women, because they have been socialized differently from men, are ill equipped to see the kinds of hurdles that must be overcome in order to be allowed inside. They lack knowledge of how the system works and where they are within it. In academia as in the business world, the rules are seldom verbalized, but the politically naive woman discovers them all too often in the act of breaking them."

In a recent paper on women and career advancement, an adviser from one of the nation's top ten schools mentioned the fact that women need to learn about the system of unwritten rules and insider behavior "not only to pursue advancement but also to even formulate goals about general career direction." They may, she suggested, need help with such matters as:

- What courses to take to prepare for a specific career or for graduate school.
- How to maximize the chances of making solid professional contacts.
- What to do to get a grant, fellowship, or other kind of financial assistance that is of an "in-house" nature.

The Mentoring Relationship

Some students feel the value of mentors lies in their ability to recognize special talents even before the student herself does. "I was a program analyst working for a county hospital and taking night courses toward a degree in public health," says one student. "One day I was meeting with my mentor to talk about grants for graduate school study, and he showed me a want-ad bulletin from one of his professional journals — 'Computer systems analyst wanted for large nursing home in Hunterdon County.' I told him it looked like they wanted someone with extensive programming experience, but he said apply anyway, that between my job experience and the computer courses I'd taken in school, I was more than qualified. Every reason I conjured up for why I wasn't qualified he countered with one that convinced me I was. Well, it turned out that I got the job, and it pays nearly double what I was making before. I realize that there's no way I would have thought myself qualified if it hadn't been for my mentor. Hearing him — a man whose professional opinion I have respected for a long time — say I could do it convinced me that I could."

The role of a mentor, according to Daniel Levinson, author of *The Seasons of a Man's Life* (Ballantine Books, New York), is one that encompasses both personal and professional development. It is one in which "a senior experienced person chooses a younger person as a protégé and teaches him [or her] specific skills, develops the protégé's intellectual abilities, intervenes to facilitate the protégé's entry and advancement, serves as host and guide to welcome the newcomer into his [or her] profession, shows him [or her] how it operates, and serves as an exemplar who embodies values and an approach to professional endeavor and personal life that the protégé can emulate."

Levinson sees the mentor as both parent and older peer, a person whose efforts and special concern push the protégé toward full realization of potential. He describes the mentoring process as spontaneous, exclusive, long lasting, and so intense that the protégé's moment of "arrival" is usually followed by a complete breach in the relationship.

"I wasn't friends with my mentor socially," says one woman who returned to school for an M.B.A. at the age of 52. "But in terms of how you define a friend, she *was* a friend. She had my best interests at heart and took me seriously in a way nobody else ever had. She gave me a sense of looking at myself as a professional. I showed her my work and she saw something in it that I hadn't even seen myself. . . . She treated me as someone who had ability, and after a while I started believing I was that person."

One of the greatest benefits of the mentoring process, according to a number of those who have been part of it, is the constant flow of "insider" information. Nowhere else, they say, can you get such knowledgeable answers to the following questions:

- Who are the most powerful and important people in the department? In the school? In the field?
- Which job markets have contacted the school for information about potential employees?
- What graduate schools offer the best programs in a particular area of specialization? Which professors have contacts with faculty at those institutions?
- How do people in the field find out about, get nominated for, and win assistantships? Fellowships? Grants? Awards? Prizes?
- What organizations are the most important to join? What conferences are the best ones to attend? Who can help you get into certain professional organizations?
- What's the best way of getting feedback on your work from certain professors? Which professors have the most to offer you?
- Which professors or administrators have contacts at places with good openings?
- What are the appropriate and accepted ways to vent grievances with specific instructors?

In addition, these women say, mentors provide more personal support of the following types:

- Individual recognition and encouragement.
- Honest criticism and informal feedback.
- Advice on how to manage the time commitments required by an academic schedule.

- Guidance as to the informal rules for advancement, as well as what and whom to avoid.
- Knowledge about the appropriate ways of making contact with important people in the field.
- Help in learning to showcase your own work.
- An understanding of how to build a circle of friends and contacts both within and outside one's academic circle.
- A perspective on long-term career planning.

A protégée can benefit from the mentor's direct intervention on her behalf or through the mentor's connections and contacts. For example, a mentor may involve the protégée in joint projects or get support for her work, introduce her to top authorities in the field, "talk up" her research to senior colleagues, or nominate her for awards and prizes.

A protégée often benefits indirectly as well. Because the mentor is respected, established, and powerful, a protégée frequently enjoys the mentor's "reflected power," which confers special status and acceptance by others. Also, she may gain from her mentor a strong sense of teaching and research as a career to which she wants to contribute in her turn.

"It was during my junior year that I became the protégée of the head of the speech and hearing department in our school," says one reentry student. "I'd asked his advice on a number of occasions and had also volunteered to be part of a certain research project he was heading, hoping to establish a closer professional relationship with him. We started meeting regularly—at least two or three times a week—and he'd give me pieces he'd torn out of journals with job contacts on them or hand me somebody's name on a piece of paper and say, 'Call them, tell them I referred you, and ask if they've got any projects going you can get hooked up with.' The most amazing thing was that all of a sudden I started getting a totally different kind of treatment from the other members of the faculty. They'd ask to see me after class to talk about research they were doing or ask *my* opinion on projects they had going. I knew what was going on had to do with my basking in Dr. Fiskett's reflected light, but it sure felt good to me."

What to Look for in Mentors

What you should look for in a mentor depends as much on your particular needs as on who is available within your department. If you're new to the school, check with students already in the department for information about individual professors. Also, talk with departmental secretaries and school advisory personnel. Finally, consider the following questions.

What is the potential mentor's achievement in key areas? What kinds of grants or fellowships has this person received? Where and how frequently has he or she been published? What panels and committees does the person serve on? What organizations does he or she belong to and in what capacities? What influence does the mentor have on shaping the department's focus in your field?

Is the mentor you are considering someone who believes whole-heartedly in your abilities? This is especially important, because a mentor's expectations can significantly enhance or undermine your self-confidence.

What has happened to this person's former protégés in terms of positions, grants, awards, etc.? Are there significant differences between what has happened to male protégés and female protégées? Have the men tended to go on to fairly good positions, while the women have drifted, failed, or had spotty employment records?

What is this person's relationship to the various groups and networks in the department, the school, and the field? Is he or she generally respected? Is his or her work known and referred to by others in the department? Is he or she known equally for academic ability and interpersonal rapport?

Is this possible mentor not only good at giving advice and direction but also able to understand your own views about your needs and goals? If unable to provide you with the information, skills, and knowledge you need, will he or she help you find someone who can? And finally, do you like this person? Can you imagine yourself in a mentoring relationship with him or her?

How to Get Mentors to Choose You

Unfortunately, as it currently operates in the school setting, the mentoring system mainly tends to bolster the professional development of men. For one thing, professors tend to choose persons most like themselves as protégés and to overlook (or exclude) newcomers. Since most professors, especially those with longtime career standing and established contacts, are male, women are frequently excluded from the mentoring system.

Also, the evidence of both experience and research indicates that male faculty members tend to see men as capable of more exceptional work than women. Male senior faculty members are more likely to give informal encouragement to men rather than women, more likely to introduce male students to influential colleagues, and more likely to pick men as teaching or research assistants.

Finally, many senior men may hesitate to mentor women because they fear rumors of sexual involvement (see the next section of this chapter). As the issue of sexual harassment becomes more and more of a campus issue and schools scurry to draft policies to clarify appropriate relationships, many women find themselves at dead ends in their search for appropriate mentors.

This is especially crippling to women who go back to school lost in a maze of conflicting feelings about the desire for achievement and with limiting preconceptions about what women should or can do. Many studies have pointed to a lack of informal guidance and sponsorship as a significant factor in explaining why so many undergraduate women avoid nontraditional fields and why they constantly downplay their potential for academic and career success.

Despite the obvious benefits, women have generally shied away from mentoring relationships for a number of reasons. To many, such relationships seem to promote a system based on favoritism rather than merit. "It just seems dishonest to accept a grant or be considered for a job *because* I happen to have a certain professional relationship with Dr. So-and-So," says a student enrolled in Adelphi University's Project EXCEL. "If I'm good enough to get the grant or the job and want it badly enough, I feel I'll get it regardless of whom I know or don't know. If I'm not good enough, well then I shouldn't have it in the first place."

Many others feel hesitant about "exploiting" personal ties for professional gain or are concerned about the potential confusion of personal and professional relationships. Some have shied away from seeking help from an "important" person; still others have been unaware of the steps they could take to initiate a mentoring relationship.

In order to make a mentoring relationship happen, you have to do more than wait passively for a senior person to notice your achievements and choose you. The following are ways in which you can make yourself highly visible as a potential protégée:

- Introduce yourself and make the first contact concerning a professional subject. Speak to the potential mentor after class, for example. Write a letter with a question that requires a response. Send your paper to a senior person whose work you respect, and request comments.

- Ask for help regarding the strengths and weaknesses of your work. Always express your appreciation for advice and criticism. Be pleasant but persistent.
- Take the initiative in putting the relationship on a more collegial basis *if* this seems appropriate. For example, if you are dealing with a professor who seems to favor informality, ask if you can call him or her by first name. Men often call professors by their first name; women rarely do.
- Try to become a research or teaching assistant, junior collaborator, proposal writer, intern, or other type of "apprentice." This will establish a context in which teaching, evaluation, and general guidance can occur naturally. It will also give you a chance to demonstrate your abilities and commitment (not to mention giving you a chance to earn a few extra dollars).

Defusing the Sexual Issue

Women's attempts to attract male mentors are frequently misinterpreted as expressions of personal interest. One woman who spent two entire semesters trying to attract a mentor said that of the few who were interested in taking her on, most thought she was propositioning them and requested that they have their first meeting in a "quiet restaurant somewhere."

There are various ways of minimizing the possibility of such a misunderstanding. You can meet with your mentor in places that discourage intimacy, such as departmental offices, labs, and other work-related settings. If possible, leave the door open. If you do meet for dinner or drinks, or on any occasion that is outside the time frame of school hours, invite a third person along. This is especially important in the initial phases, when the parameters of your relationship have as yet to be defined.

Always talk with your mentor in a professional manner, whether you are discussing personal or professional concerns. Get to know your mentor's spouse and family, and, if possible, talk about or introduce your mentor to your own spouse or romantic interest.

If your mentor suggests a sexual or romantic relationship (and you can usually trust your gut feeling on this one), confront the issue straightforwardly and firmly. You could say something like, "I'm very flattered by your attention, but I don't want to ruin the good working relationship we've developed."

Alternatives to One-on-One Mentoring

In addition to or in lieu of a "traditional" mentoring relationship, a number of alternatives exist. For instance, it is possible to have multiple mentors. Recent research suggests that men, in contrast to women, have benefited historically not only from the usual one-on-one mentoring but also from involvement in a variety of professional networks and short-term collaborative endeavors that include elements of mentoring. It has been recommended that, instead of searching for a single all-purpose mentor, women recognize the value of multiple mentoring, employing a number of people to advise, guide, support, and intervene when necessary.

In recent years, women have developed formal and informal networks throughout the business and academic communities. On campus, the network might be a group of women who meet regularly over breakfast or lunch to update each other on topics of mutual concern. It might be a formal organization of faculty members and students in a particular discipline, or it could be a group of students and like-minded faculty members who meet periodically to discuss specific academic issues. Campus networks, especially when they include students along with both senior and junior faculty members, can be significant sources of information, support, and influence.

Publications that give nitty-gritty, how-to/how-not-to information can serve as "paper mentors." These can be developed by departments, institutions, associations, or individuals. Topics covered may include such things as how to apply to graduate school, how to handle interview questions, inside sources of financial aid, and upcoming deadlines for certain contests and awards.

In many cases, mentoring relationships can be found and formed through already-established channels. These can include personal, academic, and career counseling; internships; independent-study courses; and work-study positions.

Another resource exists in courses whose aim is to teach students how to negotiate the system. These can include courses that provide an overview of the institution, those that give students a sense of how to define and meet personal academic goals, and others that survey future career or academic options. The University of South Carolina, for example, offers University 101: The Student in the University. Faculty members help students evaluate what they want to learn at the school, provide an overview of their own discipline, and introduce students to campus and community resources.

Also of use are the seminars and other programs set up to help students explore immediate academic and career options. The University of Denver offers a freshman colloquium that includes lectures, small-group meetings, and individual goal-setting interviews with faculty members, as well as a four-year career development program, in which each student works with an assigned faculty adviser and peer adviser.

There is a lot to be learned from panels or guest lectures in which successful women from a variety of fields focus on how they made academic and career choices, how being a woman affected their career development, and related issues. For example, the Center for Research on Women at Stanford University sponsors a series called "Women at the Top: The Issues They Face."

Where they exist, community-match mentoring programs are very helpful. The Center for Displaced Homemakers at Seattle Central Community College sets up information interviews and matches volunteer mentors from the business community with displaced homemakers who are almost finished with their studies and about to enter the work force. Mentors and protégées are provided with suggested topics for discussion that relate to the mentor's own career path, the skills the protégée will need, and so on. Peer mentoring programs, like the one operated by Michigan State University's counseling center, match clients with undergraduate volunteers.

Chapter

9

Jobs for the Future

If your main reason for going back to school is to prepare yourself for the job market, you're in luck. The next ten years, according to the Bureau of Labor Statistics, promises to be "a time when women will claim the largest share of the best job opportunities available."

It is said that between now and the end of the century, the U.S. economy will generate 21 million new jobs. The population, however, will grow at only two thirds of its rate in the last decade. What this means is that employers will have to turn to previously untapped groups of workers to fill existing jobs. The result will be a shift from a work force typically dominated by white males to one that includes a greater number of women and minorities. In fact, projections show that over the next eleven years, two out of every three new workers will be women (13.2 million women by the year 2000); that women, together with minorities and recent immigrants, will add 19 million new workers to the labor force; and that white, non-Hispanic men will represent less than 10 percent of all incoming workers.

By the year 2000, the number of black women in the labor force is projected to increase by 2.1 million, or 16 percent, and account for one tenth of the overall labor force growth. The number of Hispanic women will reach 5.8 million, an increase of 85 percent, more than that of white and black women combined. In addition, about one in every ten women job entrants will be of Asian, Native American, Alaskan Native, or other descent.

In addition to the increased number of working women and minorities, the labor force also will be considerably older by the year 2000. While the number of workers between the ages of 16 and 34 will decline by 4.6 million, the number between 35 and 54 will increase by 12.8 million. Half the women in the labor force will be between the ages of 35 and 54, a switch from 1986, when the majority of working women were between the ages of 25 and 44.

The Need for More Education

In many ways, women have made great gains in the work force. Although the average salary for a woman is now only 70 percent of the average salary for a man (and will still lag at 74 percent in the year 2000), women are capturing a greater share of the higher-paid jobs than in the past. In the mid-1970s, for example, women claimed about one fifth of executive, managerial, and administrative jobs. Ten years later, they were claiming a third. By the early 1980s, women accounted for 36 percent of all computer science majors; they earned 36 percent of all law degrees and 45 percent of all accountancy degrees.

The other side of the female employment picture, however, tells a radically different story. While it is true that one in every three law associates in the country's largest law firms is a woman, only one in every thirteen of these women is a partner. Eight out of ten women employed in the computer industry are clerical workers, while slightly more than one in ten is a manager. One out of three women in employment is a clerical worker (14.6 million), as opposed to one out of every seventeen men.

Most women, it seems, are concentrated at the very bottom of the professional world in an area increasingly referred to as the "pink-collar ghetto." Jobs that once represented logical stepping-stones to more desirable positions are now seen by both employers and employees as dead ends. "When I graduated from high school, I enrolled in a six-month program that taught me secretarial and office skills," says Lisa Bowman, now studying for a degree in business after spending twelve years as a clerical worker. "I thought I could start as a secretary and eventually move into a management training program. What happened was that my company, like every other office setup, started requiring advanced educational credentials before they'd place you in a training program. First it was some college, then a two-year degree. Now you have to have at least a college degree and, in some cases, an M.B.A. I realized that if I wanted to move up, I'd have to go back to school."

"There's only one road to take if you're a woman who wants to move up the career ladder, and that's advanced training," says William Johnston, Director of Workforce 2000, a study commissioned by the U.S. Department of Labor. Clerical positions, he says, are quickly becoming the new "bottom" of the job-skills curve. "As technology automates and fragments what used to be the work of one secretary or one office assistant, those jobs are increasingly seen as demanding fewer skills."

The fastest-growing jobs, he says, all tend to have higher educational requirements. In fact, of all the jobs created between 1984 and 2000, more than half will require an education beyond high school. According to Johnston, jobs that are currently in the middle of the skill distribution will be the least skilled occupations of the future, and there will be very few new jobs for the unskilled.

Over 50 percent of the 15 million new jobs created in the last ten years have been in occupational specialties that pay $400 or more per week. In the same period, low-wage jobs have actually declined. During 1988 alone, over 40 percent of the 3.1 million new jobs created were in the highest-paid occupational categories: managerial, professional, and technical.

A Changing Work Environment

To companies striving to fill an ever-increasing number of high-level positions from an ever-shrinking pool of white males, the catchword for the nineties is quickly becoming "multicultural diversity." A number of firms have already launched programs designed to prepare both managers and staff for changes that will take place naturally in the work environment as a result of the increasing number of both women and minority workers. (Such programs, by the way, are usually headed by women.)

"Nurturing diversity in the workplace makes good business sense," says Lennie Copeland, a consultant and partner in Lew Griggs Productions, San Francisco, which produced the video series "Valuing Diversity." The series was financed by thirty Fortune 500 corporations, including Aetna, Honeywell, and Xerox, and deals with overcoming stereotypes based on gender and ethnic differences. "As the number of women and minorities with corporate and buying power increases, most companies know that they have to reach out successfully to these new groups if they're going to stay in business. What better way to do that than to have a woman or a black or an Hispanic designing and heading the effort?"

Up until now, it seemed that the only efforts to move women and minorities up the corporate ladder were driven by changes originating in the legal system. Now, however, as projections show that by the year 2000 only 15 percent of the work force will consist of native white males (as opposed to 42 percent native white females, 20 percent native minorities, and 22 percent immigrants), efforts to recruit women and minorities are becoming increasingly company driven.

One of the biggest questions resulting from the increased female presence in the work force (and currently one of the most controversial job-related issues for employers) is how to handle child care. Of the nation's 6 million employers, barely 3,000 provide any help at all, and most of this help is in the form of referral assistance only.

Things may soon change, however, according to Pat Scarcelli, International Vice-President and Director of Women's Affairs for the 1.3 million members of the United Food and Commercial Workers International Union, one third of whom have children under 13. Scarcelli points to agreements like the one with Philadelphia's Acme Supermarkets, in which management voted to set aside $15 a month for each of its 2,600 unionized workers in order to pay for child-care referral services. "You're going to see a lot of agreements like this in the next few years," she says.

A more likely compromise, however (especially in the corporate setting), will be an increasing number of what are called "cafeteria packages," which ask employees to select from a broad menu the combination of benefits they prefer, up to a predetermined dollar limit. In addition to child care, such menus typically include dental coverage, pensions, and "wellness" services, as well as dozens of other health-related benefits.

Another direct result of the greater female presence in the work force is in the increasing number of companies moving toward flexible work schedules. As more and more women attempt to combine a career with the responsibilities of raising a family, the desire for greater control over the work schedule has escalated into a demand. The result is "flextime," currently available to 12 percent of the work force, which includes compressed workweeks, job sharing, and, through telecommuting, the option of working at home.

Jack Nilles of the Center for Effective Organizations estimates that more than 500,000 managerial and professional employees now work from their homes. According to the director of the National Project on Home-Based Work, an especially successful program involves 126 J. C. Penney customer-service representatives, most of them women, who handle customer queries on telephone-linked, home-based computer terminals supplied by the company.

Jobs for the Future

In 1988, women held more than 80 percent of the jobs in eleven of the twenty occupational categories that were projected to increase by more than 100,000 jobs by 1990. These twenty occupations, as shown in the table below, were expected to account for 50 percent of the projected job growth.

Occupations with Projected Increases of over 100,000, 1980–1990

	1980 Employment	Projected Growth	Percentage of Growth
1. Secretary	2,469,000	700,000	28.3
2. Nurse's aide, orderly	1,175,000	508,000	43.2
3. Janitor, sexton	2,751,000	501,000	18.2
4. Salesclerk	2,880,000	479,000	16.7
5. Cashier	1,597,000	452,000	28.4
6. Professional nurse	1,104,000	437,000	39.6
7. Truck driver	1,696,000	415,000	24.5
8. Fast-food worker	806,000	400,000	49.6
9. General office clerk	2,395,000	377,000	15.8
10. Waiter, waitress	1,711,000	360,000	21.1
11. Elementary school teacher	1,286,000	251,000	19.5
12. Kitchen helper	839,000	231,000	27.6
13. Accountant, auditor	833,000	221,000	26.5
14. Construction helper	955,000	212,000	22.2
15. Automotive mechanic	846,000	206,000	24.4
16. Blue-collar supervisor	1,297,000	206,000	15.9
17. Typist	1,067,000	187,000	17.5
18. Licensed practical nurse	522,000	185,000	35.5
19. Carpenter	970,000	173,000	17.9
20. Bookkeeper	975,000	167,000	17.2

Source: Bureau of Labor Statistics.

By contrast, the table on the next page shows the ten jobs that had the worst prospects over the same period. Most of the jobs with projected increases, however, require little more than on-the-job training. For example, service workers, the composite occupation group with the greatest increase at 5.4 million total, fall within the group of jobs that require the least skills and are overwhelmingly dominated by women.

The table on page 119 shows projected growth for twenty-five jobs requiring more advanced training. Note that some fields, such as law and engineering, are considerably better choices than others, such as college teaching.

Occupations Projected to Decrease, 1980–1990

	Number of Jobs (in thousands)		
	1980	1990	Percentage of Change
1. Postal clerk	316	310	−6
2. Clergy	296	287	−9
3. Shoe machine operator	65	54	−11
4. Compositor, typesetter	128	115	−13
5. Graduate assistant	132	108	−24
6. Servant	478	449	−29
7. College teacher	457	402	−55
8. High school teacher	1,237	1,064	−173
9. Farm laborer	1,175	940	−235
10. Farm operator	1,447	1,201	−246

Source: Bureau of Labor Statistics.

Deciding on a Career

When you are trying to decide what kind of job you might want to prepare yourself for, you should consider the following:

- **Costs and benefits.** How much schooling will you need? How much will it cost? How do those costs compare with the salary and advancement opportunities?
- **Job availability.** How many jobs are there? Where are they?
- **Working conditions.** What kind of hours will you be expected to put in? Are women highly represented in this field, or will you be breaking new ground? Are there any health and safety considerations?

Following are descriptions of eighteen occupations selected from *Jobs for the Future,* a publication of the U.S. Department of Labor's Women's Bureau. The occupations are evaluated using the preceding criteria and are grouped according to the minimum level of schooling generally required to enter a field. A majority are in service industries, including jobs in health care, banking, insurance, and education, among others. Industries in the service-producing sector are projected to generate nine out of ten new jobs between now and the year 2000.

Some Occupations Requiring a Degree, 1985–1995

	Number of Workers, 1985	Percentage of Projected Change	Numerical Increase or Decrease
Chemist	85,000	10	8,500
College or university professor	731,000	-11	-77,000
Economist	38,000	19	7,300
Engineer	1,331,000	36	480,000
Hotel manager or assistant*	83,000	26	21,000
Lawyer	490,000	36	174,000
Mathematician	21,000	19	4,000
Personnel specialist	198,000	17	34,000
Pharmacist	151,000	10	15,000
Physicist, astronomer	20,000	9	1,700
Psychologist	97,000	22	21,000
Public relations specialist	95,000	32	30,000
Purchasing agent*	189,000	19	36,000
Registered nurse**	1,377,000	33	452,000
Reporter, correspondent	69,000	19	13,000
Schoolteacher, elementary	1,381,000	20	281,000
Social worker	335,000	22	75,000
Statistician	23,000	17	3,800
Veterinarian	40,000	22	8,800
Writer, editor	191,000	28	54,000

* Strictly speaking, a college degree is not required, but most new job entrants will need one.
**Although many new nurses are obtaining college degrees, it is not a requirement; the job is listed here because training is long and specialized.

Source: Bureau of Labor Statistics.

Selected Occupations That Generally Require an Associate Degree

Computer Service Technician

Training Requirements: One to two years of post-high-school electronics or electrical training are usually necessary for hiring as a trainee; training continues with employer and includes class-room instruction and work with an experienced technician.

Training Costs: From one thousand to several thousand dollars.

Salary Range: Weekly earnings from under $270 to over $740.

Career Mobility: May become supervisor or service manager. A few technicians move into equipment sales or programming, but they need additional training in specific skills, such as programming, and may need a bachelor's degree.

Projected Growth to 1995: Much faster than average (31% or more).

Standing of Women: Underrepresented.

Work Schedule: Regular (35–40 hours, weekdays); shifts, which include evenings, late nights, weekends, on a regular basis; overtime.

Health and Safety Considerations: Hazards include minor burns and electric shock.

Dental Hygienist

Training Requirements: To obtain license, must graduate from accredited dental hygiene program and pass written and clinical exam. Most degree programs award associate degree, but some offer bachelor's and master's degrees. To get into degree program, need high school diploma and passing score on aptitude test given by American Dental Hygienists' Association.

Training Costs: From under $1,000 at some junior colleges to over $6,000 at private schools.

Salary Range: Median hourly earnings about $11.

Career Mobility: Limited mobility without additional education. Need bachelor's degree for public or school health programs, master's degree for teaching or administration. Work in a private dental office requires the least education.

Projected Growth to 1995: Faster than average (20%–30%).

Standing of Women: Traditional career for women; black and Hispanic women underrepresented.

Work Schedule: Regular (35–40 hours, weekdays); part-time; some evenings and weekends.

Health and Safety Considerations: Protective procedures must be followed in the constant use of X-ray equipment.

Legal Assistant (Paralegal)

Training Requirements: Background in legal terminology. Formal training is replacing on-the-job experience as the field gets more competitive; experience as legal secretary or other legal experience may help. Programs may last a few weeks (intensive) or four years, but most are two years, leading to certification or associate degree.

Training Costs: Vary widely.

Salary Range: Annual average from $14,400 to $27,700.

Career Mobility: Since managers are usually lawyers, mobility is limited; some firms have supervisory positions that can be reached by promotion. Can become claims or title examiner or legal investigator. Paralegals with a bachelor's degree who are seeking legal experience before entering law school can crowd out those from associate programs.

Projected Growth to 1995: Much faster than average (31% or more).

Standing of Women: Traditional career for women; black and Hispanic women slightly underrepresented.

Work Schedule: Regular (35–40 hours, weekdays); overtime.

Health and Safety Considerations: Hazards of sedentary work.

Physician's Assistant

Training Requirements: Most programs are two years. Entry is competitive and requirements vary from high school diploma to bachelor's degree, although the usual requirement is two or more years of college-level courses in science or health professions and/or prior clinical experience. Many states now require certification and regular recertification.

Training Costs: Range from free education (provided by the military) to $10,000 a year.

Salary Range: Annual salaries from about $17,000 to $39,000.

Career Mobility: Career ladders are still emerging, since the occupation has developed fairly recently. Can move from clinical work to administration, but a master's degree in public health or public administration is helpful in this case.

Projected Growth to 1995: Much faster than average (31% or more).

Standing of Women: Traditional career for women; Hispanic women underrepresented.

Work Schedule: Regular (35–40 hours, weekdays); shifts, which include evenings and weekends; overtime.

Health and Safety Considerations: Must follow safeguards against infectious diseases.

Radio/Television Technician

Training Requirements: Training includes courses in math, physics, schematic reading, and electricity, as well as practical experience. It usually takes one to two years, but some formal apprenticeships take three to four years. Some states require passing a licensing exam. Also qualified to repair stereo components, tape and videocassette recorders, video games, home security systems, and other electronic products.

Training Costs: Range from no cost to several thousand dollars.

Salary Range: Weekly earnings from about $260 to $520.

Career Mobility: In a large repair shop, can become supervisor or service manager; with training in engineering and math, can become electronics troubleshooter. More than one third are self-employed, which indicates that opportunities are good for owning one's own business, although funds will be required, as may classes in business administration.

Projected Growth to 1995: Average (11%–19%).

Standing of Women: Underrepresented.

Health and Safety Considerations: Hazards include electric shock and strain from lifting and carrying heavy equipment.

Registered Nurse

Training Requirements: Must pass state board exam and be licensed to practice. Three types of preparatory program: two-year community college and junior college programs generally leading to staff nurse positions providing bedside care; four-year bachelor's degree programs leading to clinical specializations, administration, research, and education; and three-year diploma programs in hospital-based schools (on the decline).

Training Costs: Range from $2,000 a year to over $10,000.

Salary Range: Annual earnings from about $15,000 to over $31,000.

Career Mobility: Type of degree program will affect opportunities for mobility; difficult to transfer credit from one type of program to another. Graduates of bachelor's degree programs and those with advanced degrees can move into administration, teaching, or research; a master's degree in nursing, public health, or public administration can help ensure upward mobility.

Projected Growth to 1995: Much faster than average (31% or more).

Standing of Women: Traditional career for women.

Work Schedule: Shifts, which include evenings, late nights, weekends, on regular basis; part-time; overtime.

Health and Safety Considerations: Demands of job can be strenuous; considerable walking and standing; exposure to infectious diseases; stress-related symptoms common.

Selected Occupations That Generally Require a Bachelor's Degree

Accountant/Auditor

Training Requirements: Degree in accounting or closely related field; master's degree sometimes preferred; junior accounting positions possible with associate degree. Computer training is increasingly important. Internships and work experience while in school are advantages in finding good positions.

Training Costs: Tuition may range from $1,500 to $10,000 a year.

Salary Range: Annual salaries from about $17,000 to more than $70,000 (chief managers).

Career Mobility: Usually start in assistant or junior accounting positions and move to more responsible jobs. Management accountants can move into financial management of firm (e.g., as controller, treasurer, or financial vice president). Public accountants can open their own business. Licensing as Certified Public Accountant is considered an excellent credential.

Projected Growth to 1995: Much faster than average (31% or more).

Standing of Women: Traditional career for women.

Work Schedule: Regular (35–40 hours, weekdays); part-time; overtime.

Health and Safety Considerations: Hazards of sedentary work.

Computer Programmer

Training Requirements: Combination of courses in computer programming and data processing, with courses in subject specialization of science, engineering, or business. Bachelor's degree is especially important for science and engineering applications.

Training Costs: Tuition may range up to $10,000 a year.

Salary Range: Weekly earnings from less than $285 to more than $1,000.

Career Mobility: With experience, can move from application programmer to systems programmer. Programming experience is important background for becoming a systems analyst; also possible to move into managerial positions, but may need courses in management.

Projected Growth to 1995: Much faster than average (31% or more).

Standing of Women: Traditional career for women; Hispanic women underrepresented.

123

Work Schedule: Regular (35–40 hours, weekdays); shifts, which include evenings and weekends; overtime.

Health and Safety Considerations: Possible visual-display terminal (VDT) radiation, eyestrain, backache, VDT stress; general hazards of sedentary work.

Computer Systems Analyst

Training Requirements: Degree in computer science, information systems, business, or a related mathematics/science/engineering field, plus experience as a programmer. Some employers require a master's degree. Generally specialize in either business or scientific/engineering applications.

Training Costs: Tuition may range up to $10,000 a year.

Salary Range: Weekly earnings from less than $375 to more than $970.

Career Mobility: In large departments, can move from junior systems analyst to senior or lead systems analyst; possible to move into managerial jobs within the department; more difficult to move into nontechnical management.

Projected Growth to 1995: Much faster than average (31% or more).

Standing of Women: Underrepresented.

Work Schedule: Regular (35–40 hours, weekdays); overtime.

Health and Safety Considerations: Hazards of sedentary work, possible VDT radiation, eyestrain, backache, VDT stress.

Engineer

Training Requirements: Standard entry requirement is bachelor's degree in engineering; degree in science and mathematics may also qualify the graduate for some jobs. Some specialties require a graduate degree, and some fields require licensing. The length of engineering programs varies.

Training Costs: Tuition may range up to about $12,000 a year.

Salary Range: Annual salaries from over $18,000 to more than $85,000.

Career Mobility: Assigned greater responsibility and given more complex assignments as experience is gained. Possible to move into managerial or administrative positions within engineering or nontechnical fields; graduate degree or courses in business administration may help. With law degree, engineering is excellent background for position as patent attorney (high-paid field).

Projected Growth to 1995: Much faster than average (31% or more).

Standing of Women: Underrepresented.
Work Schedule: Regular (35–40 hours, weekdays); overtime.
Health and Safety Considerations: Potential hazards vary widely with specialization.

Personnel and Labor Relations Specialist

Training Requirements: Bachelor's degree is standard but not essential. Degree can be in specialized field (personnel administration, industrial and labor relations) or relevant liberal arts field (psychology, sociology, counseling, education). Labor relations positions may require graduate work in the field, an M.B.A., or a law degree, especially for contract negotiation.
Training Costs: Tuition for liberal arts bachelor's degree programs may range from $4,000 to $12,000 a year.
Salary Range: Annual salaries from over $15,000 to nearly $75,000 (personnel director).
Career Mobility: Difficult to move beyond middle ranks of large organizations or position as head of small firm—openings are few. Some people move from personnel to labor relations, but the shift is toward labor relations specialists entering the field directly. Economics or business background, or master's or law degree, may help with advancement.
Projected Growth to 1995: Average (11%–19%).
Standing of Women: Traditional career for women.
Work Schedule: Regular (35–40 hours, weekdays); overtime.
Health and Safety Considerations: Hazards of sedentary work.

Underwriter

Training Requirements: Bachelor's degree in liberal arts or business administration; major not significant. Some companies hire people without a degree as trainees or promote underwriting clerks who show aptitude.
Training Costs: Tuition for liberal arts bachelor's degree programs may range from $4,000 to $12,000 a year.
Salary Range: Median annual salary from $24,200 to $39,000.
Career Mobility: Mainly within underwriting track; can be promoted to chief underwriter or underwriting manager; some underwriters are promoted into general management. Many opportunities available for continuing education and certification within field; credentials may count toward advancement.
Projected Growth to 1995: Faster than average (31% or more).
Standing of Women: Traditional career for women.
Work Schedule: Regular (35–40 hours, weekdays).
Health and Safety Considerations: Hazards of sedentary work.

125

Selected Occupations That Generally Required an Advanced Degree

Economist

Training Requirements: Graduate degree increasingly needed for most positions, although people with bachelor's degree can find jobs in business and government. Background should include economic theory, mathematical methods, statistical procedures, and computer applications.

Training Costs: Tuition may range up to $10,000 a year.

Salary Range: Median annual earnings from about $18,000 to more than $62,000.

Career Mobility: With master's degree, possible to move into administration, research, and planning in the public and private sectors; Ph.D. may be necessary to advance to top positions. In academia, it is increasingly difficult to obtain tenure without a doctoral degree. Background in marketing or finance may be an advantage for promotion in the private sector.

Projected Growth to 1995: Average (11%–19%).

Standing of Women: Traditional career for women; Hispanic women underrepresented.

Work Schedule: Regular (35–40 hours, weekdays); part-time; overtime. Schedules more flexible in academia.

Health and Safety Considerations: Hazards of sedentary work.

Health Services Administrator

Training Requirements: Master's degree in health administration, hospital administration, public health, public administration, business administration, or personnel administration for entry. Programs average two years beyond the bachelor's degree. Training needs may vary according to size of hiring organization.

Training Costs: Tuition may range from an average of $3,000 a year at public colleges and universities to $7,000 a year at private institutions.

Salary Range: Salaries vary widely, depending on the size of the hospital, clinic, or health-care facility. Average annual earnings of associate and chief administrators range from about $30,000 to almost $140,000.

Career Mobility: From usual beginning as department head, project director, program analyst, etc., in a large institution, may move to more responsible positions within organization or to new employer. Frequently can move to higher position in small institution. Top positions in large facilities are rare, especially in prime locations. More opportunities exist outside of hospitals (e.g., nursing homes).

Projected Growth: Faster than average (31% or more).

Standing of Women: Traditional career for women.

Work Schedule: Regular (35–40 hours, weekdays); overtime; evenings and weekends.

Health and Safety Considerations: No significant hazards, although dealing with emergency situations and other demands of health care may require long hours and induce stress or fatigue.

Lawyer

Training Requirements: Must pass exam to be admitted to the bar. To qualify for bar exam, must be graduate of accredited law school; sometimes graduates of unaccredited schools who combine law school with study in a law office or those with practical study alone can take the exam (varies by state). Bachelor's degree usually needed for entry to law school; most law programs are three years.

Training Costs: Vary widely with institution; tuition may range up to $11,000 a year.

Salary Range: Starting annual salary of recent graduates ranges from about $14,000 in some public-interest programs to over $55,000 in large law firms; average annual earnings for experienced attorneys is nearly $95,000.

Career Mobility: Usual start is in salaried position working for experienced lawyers or judges; may move to a more responsible role in the firm. Only 4 percent of law firm partners are women; still difficult to reach the top. Chain stores are opening legal services, and prepaid plans similar to health plans are developing. These pay less than traditional firms. A few lawyers become judges.

Projected Growth to 1995: Much faster than average (31% or more).

Standing of Women: Underrepresented.

Work Schedule: Regular (35–40 hours, weekdays); overtime.

Health and Safety Considerations: No significant hazards; however, may have long work hours and periods of heavy pressure that could lead to stress or fatigue.

Physician

Training Requirements: Bachelor's degree with premedicine requirements, followed by four years of medical school, a one-year internship, and two to five years of residency for specialization and licensing.

Training Costs: Tuition and fees may run from $1,500 to $28,000 a year; interns and residents earn salaries.

Salary Range: Varies with specialty, region, size of practice, and size of hospital. Stipend of residents varies but may range from $23,000 to $27,000; average income of physicians (all specialties) is $118,400.

Career Mobility: Can move from small to large institution or to more prestigious position within an institution. Can move into medical administration, based more on experience than on additional training. Can teach at a medical school. Private practice offers flexibility.

Projected Growth to 1995: Faster than average (20%–30%).

Standing of Women: Underrepresented.

Work Schedule: Regular (35–40 hours, weekdays); part-time; shifts, including evenings, late nights, and weekends, on regular basis; overtime. Schedules more flexible after training is completed.

Health and Safety Considerations: Pressures of demanding work load usually lead to fatigue and stress-related symptoms. Must follow safeguards against infectious disease.

Social Worker

Training Requirements: Master's degree is required for some entry-level positions and is necessary for advancement. Can get experience in some caseworker or group-worker positions with a bachelor's degree in social work or a liberal arts field. Half the states require licensing or registration. Graduate schools accept undergraduates with backgrounds in a variety of disciplines.

Training Costs: Tuition may range upward from $1,500 a year.

Salary Range: Average minimum salary for caseworkers with master's degree is about $22,100; experienced workers average between $24,500 and $33,800.

Career Mobility: Can become supervisor, administrator, or director of agency or program; with Ph.D., can go into teaching, research, or consulting. Small but growing number of social workers are in private practice (counseling). Courses or a degree in public health or business administration may assist in advancement.

Projected Growth to 1995: Faster than average (20%–30%).

Standing of Women: Traditional career for women.

Work Schedule: Regular (35–40 hours, weekdays); shifts, including evenings, late nights, and weekends, on regular basis; overtime.

Health and Safety Considerations: Stress resulting from frequent emergency situations with clients.

Speech Pathologist/Audiologist

Training Requirements: Master's in speech/language pathology or audiology is standard credential; bachelor's degree programs are preparation for graduate school or for job as an aide or technician. Usually need a practice certificate (administered by state) to work in public schools; thirty-one states require a license to work outside of schools.

Training Costs: Tuition may range from $3,000 to $7,000 a year.

Salary Range: Average annual salary from about $24,000 to about $38,000.

Career Mobility: Can advance to supervisory positions. Certificate of Clinical Competence, administered by the American Speech-Language-Hearing Association, can demonstrate skills for promotion.

Projected Growth to 1995: Average (11%–19%).

Standing of Women: Traditional career for women; black and Hispanic women underrepresented.

Work Schedule: Regular (35–40 hours, weekdays).

Health and Safety Considerations: No significant hazards.

Finding a Job

Looking for a job is a job in itself, the most important aspects of which are covering all the bases and organizing yourself. Some helpful practices are described in the following paragraphs.

You should have a stable base of operation, including a mailing address, a phone number, and an answering machine, where you can be reached at any time. Make sure you have the right supplies on hand: enough copies of your resume, stationery for cover letters (ideally matching the paper your resume is printed on), and envelopes with a printed return address.

List all the people whom you are going to tell you're looking for a job: friends, neighbors, former employers, former coworkers, schoolmates, professors, etc. Then tell them. Networking pays off!

List as many organizations as possible in your locality that employ people in your field. Your potential employment market can be broken down into the following four areas:

1. Carefully selected employment agencies, meaning only the ones that specialize in recruiting and placing people in your field and industry and in your salary range.
2. Want ads, not only in newspapers but also in professional journals, trade magazines, annual reports for the industry, company brochures, recruiting pamphlets, and newsletters. If you're looking for a job in business, make sure to read the business section of the newspaper in addition to the help-wanted ads. Special sections list positions available in their own specialties.
3. Resources available to women, including feminist organizations, women's centers, and women's professional and trade organizations.
4. Key employers in the field, by which is meant the individuals in organizations who make the hiring decisions, not the personnel department. For example, if you're looking for an entry-level position in marketing, call companies and ask for the name and title of the top person in marketing (just ask for the name, since you're not ready to speak to her or him just yet). Mail your resume and cover letter to that person.

Establish a timetable. Set a target date for getting a job, and make a mental commitment to it. On paper, map out your job-campaign strategy by day, by week, and by month. For example:

Week 1
- Contact personal friends and former employers.
- Compile a list of prospective employers.
- Read and follow up on want ads in the Sunday paper.

Week 2
- Mail resume and cover letter to employers on list.
- Recontact friends for referrals.
- Send resume and cover letter to friends' referrals.
- Visit employment agencies.
- Research and compile information on employment prospects in the field.

Week 3
- Contact employers from the want ads you answered during Week 1.
- Phone employers to arrange interviews.
- Mail resume to employment prospects.

Get information about job trends and possibilities in your geographic area. The state employment security agency publishes reports on projected employment in your area and on other subjects concerning the local labor market. The State Occupational Information Coordinating Committee also can help in your search for information about careers or job prospects in your state or locality. Consult the telephone directory for the location of these agencies, or consult the *Occupational Outlook Handbook* in the public library or at your school.

An excellent source of local job data is the regional office of the U.S. Department of Labor's Women's Bureau. Its staff can answer questions about how many women in your locality work in a particular occupation or industry, about the nature and location of organizations concerned with training and employment issues affecting women, or about any other issues regarding the employment of women in your state or region. Appendix G is a list of the regional offices of the Women's Bureau.

Appendix A

Gaining Academic Acceptance for Nontraditional Learning

Following is a three-point strategy for gaining academic credit for formal learning acquired outside the traditional college environment. It comes from the Program on Noncollegiate Sponsored Instruction (PONSI) of the American Council on Education (ACE).

1. Know what factors affect a college's decision to award credit.

Does the subject area fit? Does the content of your course fit into your college's degree curriculum? For example, if your course was in computer programming and you are enrolled or about to enroll in a business degree program, does the business curriculum include programming? If so, did your course cover the topics required in the college course? If it did, be prepared to discuss how your course is a suitable substitute. If it didn't, find out if you can use the course as an elective subject. If you don't know whether your course content fits, you should try to find out by reviewing the college catalog or other materials. The more information you have, the more likely you will be able to negotiate your request successfully.

Do you have academically credible information and documentation? One reason colleges do not accept noncollegiate courses is that these courses are not described in academic terms or on academic schedules. Be prepared to show your college an academic course description and some kind of official transcript. Official transcripts should contain course titles, numbers, dates, duration, location, and final marks.

What general restriction does your college place on outside learning? Most colleges set a limit on the number of credits they will grant for studies not completed on their campus. Find out what this limit is (30 credits, 60 credits, etc.) and whether you have already exceeded it with transfer credits from other sources. (Limits on transfer credits are usually stated in the school catalog.) If you have *not* reached the limit, you will have a much better chance of having your courses accepted.

2. Find out which official at your college makes the decision to award credit for transfer courses.

The appropriate person varies from college to college. It could be that you will need to deal with the chairperson of the department that offers your degree program, a member of the faculty transcript committee, the dean of your particular academic area (e.g., engineering, business, arts and sciences), the admissions officer, the registrar, or the faculty adviser.

133

If you are already enrolled at your college, try contacting your faculty adviser or department chairperson and ask her or him to give you the name of the person in charge of granting credit for transfer courses. Don't be surprised if you run into some skepticism or resistance at first because your courses are noncollegiate. However, if you have "done your homework," as described in step 1, you should be able to provide the rationale needed to overcome much of the skepticism.

If you are not yet enrolled at the college of your choice, call the admissions office, tell them what degree program you are interested in, and ask for the name of the person who makes the decision about awarding transfer credit for that particular degree program. As in the case of students who are already enrolled, you should not be surprised if you initially meet with some skepticism or resistance over accepting your credits.

3. What to do if your courses are rejected.

First find out the reason for the rejection. Is it because the course content does not fit into the curriculum and you have no room left for elective credit in your degree program? Or have you already reached the limit of transfer credit that the college will accept? If the answer is yes in either case, it is unlikely that you can do much without actually changing degree programs or colleges.

If, however, the rejection is the result of a departmental or institutional policy to accept no noncollegiate credit, you might want to consider writing a carefully thought-out letter of appeal to the academic dean or provost at the college. (Be sure to address the issues mentioned in step 1.) In addition, you should contact the American Council on Education, Program on Noncollegiate Sponsored Instruction, One Dupont Circle, Washington, DC 20036, 202-939-9433, and ask a member of the staff to provide the recipient of your letter with additional information on the PONSI process for acceptance of credit.

If the answer is still no, you have two final alternatives. One is, of course, to continue your degree application or studies at that college and forget about receiving credit for your courses. Your second choice would be to shop around. (ACE lists over 1,500 accredited colleges and universities that accept its credit recommendations.)

Contact other colleges in your area for their policies on PONSI courses, or consider another alternative, an external degree program of the sort offered by Thomas A. Edison State College or the Regents College Degrees and Examinations program of the State University of New York. Both programs recognize PONSI-evaluated courses as well as accredited college courses, which means that you can continue taking courses at your local college if you like. For more information, contact Thomas A. Edison State College, 101 West State Street, CN 545, Trenton, NJ 08625, 609-984-1121, or Regents College Degrees and Examinations, Cultural Education Center, State University of New York, Albany, NY 12330, 518-474-3703.

Appendix B

Selected Colleges Offering Accredited Correspondence Courses

For information about the correspondence courses offered at these colleges and universities, contact the person whose name appears on the first line of each address.

Ralph Rowley, Department
 Chairman
Independent Study
206 Harmon Continuing
 Education Building
Brigham Young University
Provo, UT 84602
Telephone: 801-378-2868

Frank DiSilvestro, Associate
 Director for Extended Studies
 for Independent Study
Independent Study Program
Owen Hall 001
Indiana University
Bloomington, IN 47405
Telephone: 812-335-3693

Don Hammons, Director
Independent Study by
 Correspondence
Louisiana State University
Baton Rouge, LA 70803
Telephone: 504-388-3171

Dr. Richard Moffitt, Director of
 Independent Study
Tupper Hall 303
Ohio University
Athens, OH 45701
Telephone: 614-594-6721

Dr. Charles E. Feasley, Director
Independent and
 Correspondence Study
 Department
001 Classroom Building
Oklahoma State University
Stillwater, OK 74078
Telephone: 405-624-6390

Dr. David Mercer, Director of
 Independent Learning
Department of Independent
 Study by Correspondence
128 Mitchell Building
Pennsylvania State University
University Park, PA 16802
Telephone: 814-865-5403

Arny Reichler, Director
External Degree Programs
Roosevelt University
430 South Michigan Avenue
Chicago, IL 60005
Telephone: 312-341-3866

William Seaton, Director
Guided Study Program
Thomas A. Edison State College
101 West State Street, CN 545
Trenton, NJ 08625
Telephone: 609-292-6317

Ms. Terry McNally
Independent Study, Department
NN
University of California
2223 Fulton Street
Berkeley, CA 94720
Telephone: 415-642-4124

Harold Markowitz Jr., Director
Department of Independent
Study
Division of Continuing
Education
University of Florida
1938 West University Avenue,
Room 1
Gainesville, FL 32603
Telephone: 904-392-1711

Dr. Robert W. Batchellor, Head
Guided Independent Study
Division
104 Illini Hall
University of Illinois
725 South Wright Street
Champaign, IL 61820
Telephone: 217-333-1321 Ext.
3758

Phyllis Hopp, Office Coordinator
Guided Correspondence Study
W400 Seashore Hall
University of Iowa
Iowa City, IA 52242
Telephone: 319-353-4963

Nancy Colyer, Director of
Independent Study
Division of Continuing
Education
University of Kansas
Lawrence, KS 66045
Telephone: 913-864-4792

Dr. Earl Pfansteil, Director
Independent Study Program
Frazee Hall, Room 1
University Extension
University of Kentucky
Lexington, KY 40506-0031
Telephone: 606-257-3466

Deborah Nelson, Associate
Director
Department of Independent
Study
45 Westbrook Hall
University of Minnesota
77 Pleasant Street, SE
Minneapolis, MN 55455
Telephone: 612-373-3803

Dr. Monty McMahon, Director
Department of Independent
Study
Division of Continuing Studies
269 Nebraska Center for
Continuing Education
University of Nebraska–Lincoln
Lincoln, NE 68583-0900
Telephone: 402-472-1926

Dr. Donald F. Kaiser, Director of
Independent Study
University of Wisconsin
Extension
432 North Lake Street
Madison, WI 53706
Telephone: 608-263-2055

Appendix C

Scholarships Offered by the AFL-CIO

The following scholarships mainly are offered only to members of the sponsoring union or their dependents. For further information, write to the AFL-CIO Department of Education, Room 407, 815 16th Street, NW, Washington, DC 20006.

ALASKA
Kenai Peninsula Federation of Teachers: two scholarships of $500 each.

ARKANSAS
United Steelworkers of America, District 37: seven scholarships of from $500 to $800 each.

CALIFORNIA
American Federation of Teachers
  Local 61: five scholarships of $400 each.
  Local 1936: four book scholarships of $150 each and one adult-education scholarship of $50.
Bakery, Confectionery and Tobacco Workers International Union, Local 37: three scholarships of $1,000 each.
Communications Workers of America, Local 9510: three scholarships of $1,000 each.
International Association of Machinists and Aerospace Workers, Local 1305: one scholarship of $1,000.
International Brotherhood of Electrical Workers, Local 1245: one scholarship and one grant of $500 each.
International Union of Operating Engineers, Local 3: two scholarships of $1,000 each and two of $500 each.
Laborers' International Union of North America, Local 652: six scholarships of $1,000 each and two of $500 each.
National Association of Letter Carriers, Branch 1100: two scholarships of $1,000 each.
The Newspaper Guild: one scholarship of $500.
Service Employees International Union
  California State Council: three scholarships of $750 each.
  Local 700: one scholarship of $500.

CONNECTICUT
American Postal Workers Union, Connecticut State Postal Workers Union: two scholarships of $1,000 each.
United Automobile, Aerospace and Agricultural Implement Workers of America International Union, Local 626: Scholarships of $500; number varies.

United Brotherhood of Carpenters and Joiners of America, Local 210: two scholarships of $1,000 each.

United Food and Commercial Workers International Union, Local 371: four scholarships of $1,000 each.

COLORADO

International Association of Machinists and Aerospace Workers, Local Lodge R-1338: one scholarship of $2,000.

DISTRICT OF COLUMBIA

American Federation of Teachers, Local 327: four scholarships of $2,000 each.

International Brotherhood of Electrical Workers, Local 1245: one scholarship and one grant of $500 each.

Office and Professional Employees International Union, Local 327: one scholarship of $200.

FLORIDA

International Association of Machinists and Aerospace Workers, Local Lodge 2061: one scholarship of $1,000.

GEORGIA

International Brotherhood of Electrical Workers, Local 613: Number and amount of scholarships vary.

HAWAII

American Federation of State, County and Municipal Employees, Local 152 (Hawaii Government Employees Association): six scholarships of $1,000 each.

American Federation of Teachers, Local 1127: seven scholarships of $250 each.

ILLINOIS

Amalgamated Clothing and Textile Workers Union, Chicago and Central States Joint Board: Number of scholarships varies; $700 each.

American Federation of State, County and Municipal Employees, Council 31: two scholarships of $750 each.

American Federation of Teachers, Local 1: ten scholarships of $1,000 each.

Bloomington and Normal Trades and Labor AFL-CIO: Stanley Johnson scholarship; amount varies.

International Union of Bricklayers and Allied Craftsmen, Local 21: five scholarships of $500 each.

The Newspaper Guild, Local 86, Peoria: six to eight scholarships of $100 each for a summer journalism workshop.

Service Employees International Union
Local 11: fifteen scholarships of $500 each.
Local 25: two scholarships of $1,000 each.

INDIANA

United Steelworkers of America
District 31, Local 31: one scholarship of $1,000.
Local 1011: one scholarship of $1,000.

IOWA

American Federation of Government Employees, Local 1226: one scholarship of $500.

United Food and Commercial Workers International Union, Local
1169-P: two scholarships of $300 each.

KANSAS
International Association of Machinists and Aerospace Workers, AERO
Lodge 834: two scholarships per semester of $225 each.
United Brotherhood of Carpenters and Joiners of America, Local 168: up
to three scholarships of $150 each.
United Rubber, Cork, Linoleum and Plastic Workers of America, Local
307: two scholarships of $1,000 and $750.

KENTUCKY
Service Employees International Union, Local 557: number of
scholarships varies.

MARYLAND
American Federation of Government Employees, Local 1923: one
scholarship of $500 a year for four years.
National Association of Letter Carriers, Branch 176: four scholarships of
$500 each.
United Automobile, Aerospace and Agricultural Implement Workers of
America International Union, Region 8, Baltimore: three awards
ranging from $400 to $1,000.
United Brotherhood of Carpenters and Joiners of America, Local 1145:
two scholarships of $600 each and two of $500 each.
United Food and Commercial Workers International Union, Local 27: five
scholarships of $2,000 each.
United Steelworkers of America, District 8: four scholarships of $500
each.

MASSACHUSETTS
International Ladies Garment Workers Union
Local 75: 1 scholarship of $400.
Local 226: 1 scholarship of $400.
Local 324: 1 scholarship of $400.
Local 341: 1 scholarship of $400.
Local 361: 1 scholarship of $500.
Retail, Wholesale and Department Store Union, Leominster Joint Board:
one scholarship of $2,500 and one of $1,500.
United Brotherhood of Carpenters and Joiners of America: two
scholarships of $2,000 each.

MICHIGAN
American Federation of Teachers, Local 231: one scholarship of $500.
Public Employees International Union, Local 992, Gogebic County: two
scholarships of $300 each.
Service Employees International Union
Local 466M: four scholarships of $500 each.
Wayne County Sheriffs, Local 502: six scholarships of $600 each.
United Automobile, Aerospace and Agricultural Workers of America
International Union
Region 1: four scholarships of $500 each.
Region 1B: one scholarship of $300 and two of $1,000 each.
Region 1D: one scholarship of $1,000 and two of $500 each.

Local 160: four scholarships of $1,000 each.
Local 724: one scholarship of $1,000.

MINNESOTA

American Federation of State, County and Municipal Employees, Local 1949: two scholarships of $300 each.
American Federation of Teachers
Minnesota Federation: two scholarships of $1,000 each.
Local 122: multiple scholarships of $500 each.
Local 1802: one scholarship of $200.
Local 2242: one scholarship of $200.
International Brotherhood of Electrical Workers, Local 110: one scholarship of $500 for four years.
International Union of Electronic, Electrical, Salaried, Machine and Furniture Workers, AFL-CIO District 11: three scholarships of $500 each.
Service Employees International Union, Local 284: three scholarships of $300 each.
United Association of Journeymen and Apprentices of the Plumbing and Pipe Fitting Industry of the United States and Canada, Local 15: one scholarship of $1,000.
United Brotherhood of Carpenters and Joiners of America, Twin Cities Carpenters District Council: one scholarship of $800 and fifteen of $750 each.
United Food and Commercial Workers International Union, Region 13: three scholarships of $1,000 each.

MISSOURI

American Federation of Teachers, Local 691: two scholarships of $500 each.
International Association of Machinists and Aerospace Workers
Local Lodge 778: one scholarship of $1,000.
Local Lodge R312: one scholarship of $2,000.
Laborers' International Union of North America, Local 42: two scholarships of $2,000 each.
Service Employees International Union, Local 50: five scholarships of $1,000 each.
United Association of Journeymen and Apprentices of the Plumbing and Pipe Fitting Industry of the United States and Canada, Local 533: two scholarships of $4,000 each.
United Steelworkers of America
District 34: two scholarships of $4,000 each.
Local 1958: two scholarships of $2,000 each.

MONTANA

American Federation of Teachers
Local 332: four scholarships of $500 each.
Local 3183: one scholarship of $300.
Local 3778: three scholarships of $100 each.
Oil, Chemical and Atomic Workers International Union, Local 2493: two scholarships of $200 each.

NEW HAMPSHIRE

American Federation of Teachers, Local 1044: one scholarship of $1,000.

Professional and Technical Engineers, Local 4, Portsmouth: one scholarship of $500.

NEW JERSEY

International Brotherhood of Electrical Workers, Local 456: one scholarship of $4,000.

Professional and Technical Engineers, Local 194: one scholarship of $500 a year for four years.

United Food and Commercial Workers International Union, Local 464A: three scholarships of $1,000 each for four years and twelve of $1,000 each for one year.

United Paperworkers International Union, Local 300: two scholarships of $3,000 each.

United Steelworkers of America, District 9: one scholarship of $1,600.

NEW YORK

Albany

Civil Service Employees Association, Inc., AFSCME, AFL-CIO, Local 1000: eighteen scholarships of $500 each.

International Association of Fire Fighters: two scholarships of $600 each.

New York State Public Employees Federation (AFT/SEIU): ten scholarships of up to $4,000 each.

Public Employees Federation (AFT/SEIU)
  Local 4053: two scholarships of $500 each.
  Local 4053, Division 177: two scholarships of $500 each.

Albion

United Brotherhood of Carpenters and Joiners of America, New York State Council of Carpenters: one scholarship of $500.

Amsterdam

American Federation of Teachers, Local 1150: three scholarships of $50 each.

Bayport

American Federation of Teachers: five scholarships of $500 each.

Buffalo/Rochester

International Brotherhood of Painters and Allied Trades, District Council 4: four scholarships of $1,000 each.

United Automobile, Aerospace and Agricultural Implement Workers of America International Union
  Local 424: one scholarship of $1,000.
  Local 774: five scholarships of $250 each.
  Local 897: five scholarships of $1000 each.

Cheektowaga

Aluminum, Brick and Glass Workers International Union, Local 222: one scholarship of $500.

Dobbs Ferry

American Federation of Teachers, Local 1534: one scholarship of $1,000.

Garden City

American Federation of Teachers, Local 3150: fifteen scholarships varying from $250 to $3,000 each.

Geneva

International Brotherhood of Electrical Workers, Local 840: number and amount of scholarships vary.

Greenburgh

American Federation of Teachers, Local 1788: two scholarships of $100 each.

Jamaica

International Association of Machinists and Aerospace Workers: one scholarship of $1,000.

Newburgh

International Association of Fire Fighters, Local 589: one scholarship of $500.

New York City

Amalgamated Clothing and Textile Workers Union
New York Joint Board: twenty scholarships of $3,000 each.
Service and Allied Industries Joint Board: Number of scholarships varies; current amount is $3,600 each.
American Federation of Musicians of the United States and Canada, Local 99: Number of scholarships varies; amount ranges up to $600 each.
American Federation of State, County and Municipal Employees, District 37: thirty-five full- and part-time tuition scholarships.
American Federation of Teachers, UFT, Local 2: 300 scholarships of $4,000 each.
Communications Workers of America, Local 1180: tuition reimbursement for members of the local.
Enterprise Association
Metal Trades Branch, Local 638: four scholarships of $500 each.
Steamfitters, Local 638: six scholarships of $4,000 each.
Graphic Communications International Union, Local 51: four scholarships of $2,000 each.
Hospital and Health Care Employees International Union, 1199 National Benefit Fund for Hospital and Health Care Employees: 912 scholarships, ranging from $175 to $3,000 each.
Hotel Employees and Restaurant Employees International Union, Local 6: one scholarship of $1,000 and two of $500 each.
International Association of Bridge, Structural and Ornamental Iron Workers, Metal Lathers, Local 46: ten scholarships of $4,000 each.
International Brotherhood of Electrical Workers, Local 3: thirty scholarships of $8,000 each.
International Longshoremen's Association, Local 1814: three scholarships of $5,000 each.
International Union of Electronic, Electrical, Salaried, Machine and Furniture Workers, Local 463: from two to four scholarships of $1,000 each for four years.
International Union of Operating Engineers, Local 30, 30A, 30B, 30C, 30D: two scholarships of $500 each per semester.
International Union of Operating Engineers, Stationary Engineers, Local 30: two scholarships of $500 each per semester.
Marine Engineers Beneficial Association, District 2: eighty-one scholarships, ranging from $1,000 to $2,000 each.
National Association of Letter Carriers, Branch 36: four scholarships of $2,000 each.

The Newspaper Guild, Local 3: eighteen scholarships of from $1,000 to $2,000 each.

The New York Building Industry, Building Contractors Association: twenty scholarships of $8,000 each.

New York Hotel and Motel Trades Council, AFL-CIO: thirty-four scholarships of $2,000 each.

Retail, Wholesale and Department Store Union, Local 338: ten scholarships of $1,000 each.

Service Employees International Union

    Amalgamated Jewelry, Diamond and Watchcase Workers Union, Local I-J: four scholarships of $700 each.

    Metal Spinners Industry-Wide Pension Plan: two scholarships of $1,000 each.

    New York Taxi Drivers Union, Local 3036: number of scholarships varies—up to four of $7,000 each, two of $5,000 each, five of $1,000 each, and one of $500.

    Local 32B-J: one undergraduate scholarship of $2,000 and one professional or doctoral-level scholarship of $32,000.

    Local 32E: five scholarships of $1,000 each for four years.

    Local 49E: one scholarship of $1,000 and one of $500.

    Local 74: one graduate scholarship of $20,000, one undergraduate scholarship of $20,000, ten scholarships of $2,000 each, twenty-one of $1,000 each, four of $8,000 each, and one of $10,000.

    Local 144: four scholarships of $4,000 each.

    Local 365: two scholarships of $2,000 each.

Sheet Metal Workers' International Association, Local 28: three scholarships of $4,000 each and nine of $3,000 each.

United Automobile, Aerospace and Agricultural Implement Workers of America International Union, Local 259: four scholarships of $500 each.

United Food and Commercial Workers International Union

    Local 50-234: four scholarships of $400 each.

    Local 174: one scholarship; amount varies.

    Local 342: number of scholarships varies; amount varies from $200 to $2,000 each.

United Garment Workers of America

    International Ladies Garment Workers Union, Local 23-25: fifty scholarships of $1,000 each.

    Knitgood Workers Union, Local 155: fifteen scholarships of $1,000 each.

Utility Workers Union of America, Local 1-2: twenty-two scholarships of $1,000 each.

Plainview

American Federation of School Administrators, Local 12: six scholarships of $500 each.

Port Chester

American Federation of Teachers: seventeen scholarships, ranging from $50 to $500 each.

Rochester

United Brotherhood of Carpenters and Joiners of America, Local 85: one
scholarship of $500 and one of $1,000.

Schenectady

American Federation of Teachers, Local 2698: one or two scholarships of
$800 each.

International Union of Electronic, Electrical, Salaried, Machine and
Furniture Workers, Local 301: two scholarships of $500 each for
study at a two-year college; two of $1,000 each for study at a four-
year college.

Professional and Technical Engineers: one scholarship of $500.

Syracuse

American Federation of Teachers, Local 2999: one scholarship of $3,000
and one of $250.

Yonkers

American Federation of Teachers, Local 860: five scholarships of $500
each.

Yorktown Heights

American Federation of Teachers, Local 1724: two scholarships of $650
each.

NORTH CAROLINA

Communications Workers of America
Local 3060: two scholarships of $250 each and two of $500 each.
Local 3603: one scholarship of $1,000, one of $750, and one of $500.

NORTH DAKOTA

International Brotherhood of Electrical Workers, Local 1426: one
scholarship of $200.

OHIO

American Federation of Teachers, Local 8033: three scholarships of $500
each.

International Association of Machinists and Aerospace Workers, Local
Lodge 1280: one scholarship of $1,000.

International Union of Electronic, Electrical, Salaried, Machine and
Furniture Workers, District Council 7: fifteen scholarships of $750
each.

United Automobile, Aerospace and Agricultural Implement Workers of
America International Union
Region 2A: one Walter P. Reuther scholarship of up to $1,000.
Region 2B: six Richard Gosser scholarships of $4,000 each.
Local 402: fourteen John Minchin scholarships of $500 each.

OKLAHOMA

American Federation of Teachers, Local 2309: two scholarships of $500
each.

OREGON

American Federation of Musicians of the United States and Canada,
Local 99: number varies; amount ranges up to $600 each.

Service Employees International Union, Local 503: ten to fifteen
scholarships of from $375 to $750 each.

PENNSYLVANIA

Amalgamated Clothing and Textile Workers Union, Eastern

Pennsylvania Clothing Workers Joint Board: sixteen scholarships of $3,000 each.
American Federation of State, County and Municipal Employees, Local 2360: four scholarships of $100 each and five of $50 each.
American Federation of Teachers
    Local 3: thirty-five scholarships of $100 each.
    Local 1417: six scholarships of $200 each.
    Local 1421: Number of scholarships of $500 each varies.
Glass, Molders, Pottery, Plastics and Allied Workers International Union, Local 18: four scholarships of $2,500 each.
Hotel Employees and Restaurant Employees International Union, Local 634: nine scholarships of $800 each.
International Association of Machinists and Aerospace Workers
    Lodge 43: one scholarship of $1,000.
    Lodge 928: three scholarships of $50 each.
International Brotherhood of Electrical Workers, Local 1600: five scholarships of $1,000 each.
International Brotherhood of Painters and Allied Trades, Local 252: one scholarship of $500.
International Ladies Garment Workers Union
    Local 93: three scholarships of $500 each.
    Locals 185-306-351: two scholarships of $500 each.
    Locals 234 and 243: one scholarship of $750, five of $500 each, and four of $300 each.
International Union of Electronic, Electrical, Salaried, Machine and Furniture Workers, District 1: three scholarships of $500 each.
Service Employees International Union, Local 668: twenty scholarships of $100 each.
United Paperworkers International Union, Local 286; seven scholarships of $1,000 each.
United Steelworkers of America
    District 7: eight scholarships of $3,000 each.
    District 20 North: nine scholarships of $1,500 each.
    Local 3657: four scholarships of $800 each.

RHODE ISLAND
American Federation of State, County and Municipal Employees, Council 94: ten scholarships of $300 each.
American Federation of Teachers, Local 951: twenty scholarships of $300 each.
The Newspaper Guild, Local 41: three scholarships of $2,000 each.

TEXAS
Paperworkers International Union, Local 1068: two scholarships of $500 each.

VERMONT
American Federation of Teachers, Local 8043: three scholarships; amount varies.
United Steelworkers of America, District 1, Local 4: five scholarships of $400 each.

VIRGINIA
International Longshoremen's Association, Local 846: ten scholarships of $500 each.

WASHINGTON

American Federation of State, County and Municipal Employees
Washington Federation of State Employees: one scholarship of $200.
Local 443: two scholarships of $500 each and one of $100 per quarter.

WEST VIRGINIA

United Steelworkers of America, District 23: eight scholarships of $2,400 each.

WISCONSIN

Allied Industrial Workers of America International Union
Region 9, Council 13: one Francis Jeffords scholarship of $750.
Region 9, Local 232: one scholarship of $1,000.
American Federation of State, County and Municipal Employees
Council 24: one scholarship of $1,000 and two of $500 each.
Council 40: four scholarships of $1,000 each, two of $500 each, one of $500 for a physically handicapped student, and one of $500 for a special education student.
American Federation of Teachers, Local 3307: one scholarship of $1,000.
International Association of Machinists and Aerospace Workers
Lodge 34: five scholarships of $500 each.
Local Lodge C1493: one scholarship of $2,000.
United Steelworkers of America, District 32, Local 1343: two scholarships of $500 each.

Appendix D

Sources of Information on Federal Student Loans and State Aid

ALABAMA
Alabama Commission on Higher Education, Suite 221, One Court Square, Montgomery, AL 36197-0001 (205-269-2700).

ALASKA
Alaska Commission on Postsecondary Education, 400 Willoughby Avenue, Box FP, Juneau, AK 99811 (907-465-2854).

ARIZONA
Federal student loans: Arizona Educational Loan Program, Suite 621, 2600 North Central Avenue, Phoenix, AZ 85012 (602-252-5793).
State aid: Commission for Postsecondary Education, Suite 1407, 3030 North Central Avenue, Phoenix, AZ 85012 (602-255-3109).

ARKANSAS
Federal student loans: Student Loan Guarantee Foundation, 219 South Victory Street, Little Rock, AR 72201-1884 (501-372-1491).
State aid: Arkansas Department of Higher Education, 1220 West Third Street, Little Rock, AR 72201-1904 (501-371-1441).

CALIFORNIA
Federal student loans: California Educational Loan Program Processing Center, Suite 193, 3332 Matherfield Road, Rancho Cordova, CA 95670 (800-548-2357).
State aid: California Student Aid Commission, P.O. Box 945625, Sacramento, CA 94245-0625 (916-323-0435).

COLORADO
Federal student loans: Colorado Student Loan Program, Suite 500, 11990 Grant, North Glenn, CO 80233 (303-450-9333).
State aid: Colorado Commission on Higher Education, Second Floor, Colorado Heritage Center, 1300 Broadway, Denver, CO 80203 (303-866-2723).

CONNECTICUT
Federal student loans: Connecticut Student Loan Foundation, P.O. Box 1009, Rocky Hill, CT 06067.
State aid: Connecticut Department of Higher Education, 61 Woodland Street, Hartford, CT 06105-2391 (203-566-2618).

DELAWARE

Federal student loans: Delaware Higher Education Loan Program, Delaware Postsecondary Education Commission, Fourth Floor, Carvel State Office Building, 820 North French Street, Wilmington, DE 19801 (302-571-6055).

State aid: 302-571-3240.

DISTRICT OF COLUMBIA

Federal student loans: Higher Education Loan Program of Washington, D.C., Suite 1050, 1030 15th Street, NW, Washington DC 20005 (202-289-4500).

State aid: Office of Postsecondary Education Research and Assistance, D.C. Department of Human Services, Suite 600, 1331 H Street, NW, Washington, DC 20005 (202-727-3688).

FLORIDA

Office of Student Financial Assistance, Department of Education, Knott Building, Tallahassee, FL 32399 (904-488-8093 for federal student loans; 904-488-6181 for state aid).

GEORGIA

Georgia Student Finance Authority, Suite 200, 2082 East Exchange Place, Tucker, GA 30084 (404-493-5468 for federal student loans; 404-493-5444 for state aid).

HAWAII

Federal student loans: Hawaii Education Loan Program, P.O. Box 22187, Honolulu, HI 96822-0187 (808-536-3731).

State aid: State Postsecondary Education Commission, 209 Bachman Hall, University of Hawaii, 2444 Dole Street, Honolulu, HI 96822 (808-948-8213).

IDAHO

Federal student loans: Student Loan Fund of Idaho, P.O. Box 730, Fruitland, ID 83619 (208-452-4058).

State aid: State Board of Education, Room 307, 650 West State Street, Boise, ID 83720 (208-334-2270).

ILLINOIS

Illinois State Scholarship Commission, 106 Wilmot Road, Deerfield, IL 60015 (708-948-8550).

INDIANA

State Student Assistance Commission, 964 North Pennsylvania Street, Indianapolis, IN 46204 (317-232-2366 for federal student loans; 317-232-2350 for state aid).

IOWA

Iowa College Aid Commission, 210 Jewett Building, Ninth and Grand, Des Moines, IA 50309 (515-281-4890 for federal student loans; 515-281-3501 for state aid).

KANSAS

Federal student loans: Higher Education Assistance Foundation, Suite 600, 6800 College Boulevard, Overland Park, KS 66211-1532 (913-345-1300).

State aid: Kansas Board of Regents, Suite 609, Capital Tower, 400 SW Eighth, Topeka, KS 66603-3911 (913-296-3517).

KENTUCKY

Kentucky Higher Education Assistance Authority, 1050 U.S. 127 South, Frankfort, KY 40601 (502-564-2427).

LOUISIANA

Governor's Special Commission on Education Services, P.O. Box 91202, Baton Rouge, LA 70821-9202 (504-922-1011).

MAINE

Division of Higher Education Services, Department of Educational and Cultural Services, State House Station 119, Augusta, ME 04333 (207-289-2183).

MARYLAND

Federal student loans: Higher Education Loan Corporation, Room 305, 2100 Guilford Avenue, Baltimore, MD 21218 (301-333-6555).

State aid: Maryland State Scholarship Administration, 16 Francis Street, Annapolis, MD 21401 (301-974-5370).

MASSACHUSETTS

Higher Education Assistance Corporation, Room 600, 150 Causeway Street, Boston, MA 02114 (617-727-9420).

MICHIGAN

Federal student loans: Michigan Guaranty Agency, Michigan Department of Education, P.O. Box 30047, Lansing, MI 48909 (517-373-0760).

State aid: Student Financial Assistance Services, Michigan Department of Education, P.O. Box 30008, Lansing, MI 48909 (517-373-3394).

MINNESOTA

Federal student loans: Minnesota Higher Education Assistance Foundation, Suite 500, 85 East Seventh Steet, St. Paul, MN 55101 (612-227-7661).

State aid: Minnesota Higher Education Coordinating Board, Suite 400, Capitol Square Building, 550 Cedar Street, St. Paul, MN 55101 (612-296-3974).

MISSISSIPPI

Federal student loans: Mississippi Stafford Loan Program, 3825 Ridgewood Road, P.O. Box 342, Jackson, MS 39205-0342 (601-982-6663).

State aid: Student Financial Aid, Board of Trustees of State Institutions of Higher Learning, P.O. Box 2336, Jackson, MS 39225-2336 (601-982-6570).

MISSOURI

Coordinating Board for Higher Education, P.O. Box 1438, Jefferson City, MO 65102 (314-751-3940).

MONTANA

Office of the Commissioner of Higher Education, Montana University System, 35 South Last Chance Gulch, Helena, MT 59620-3104 (406-444-6594).

NEBRASKA

Federal student loans: Higher Education Assistance Foundation, Suite 304, Cornhusker Bank Building, 11th and Cornhusker Highway, Lincoln, NE 68521 (402-476-9129).

State aid: each college and university in Nebraska administers aid through its own financial aid office.

NEVADA

Federal student loans: Nevada Educational Loan Program, United Student Aid Funds, Inc., 8085 Knue Road, P.O. Box 50827, Indianapolis, IN 46250 (800-428-9250).

State aid: each college and university in Nevada administers aid through its own financial aid office.

NEW HAMPSHIRE

Federal student loans: New Hampshire Higher Education Assistance Foundation, P.O. Box 877, Concord, NH 03301 (603-225-6612).

State aid: New Hampshire Postsecondary Education Commission, 2½ Beacon Street, Concord, NH 03301 (603-271-2555).

NEW JERSEY

Office of Student Assistance, 4 Quakerbridge Plaza, CN 540, Trenton, NJ 08625 (in New Jersey, 800-792-8670).

NEW MEXICO

Federal student loans: New Mexico Educational Assistance Foundation, P.O. Box 27020, Albuquerque, NM 87125-7020 (505-345-3371).

State aid: Commission on Higher Education, 1068 Cerrillos Road, Santa Fe, NM 87501-4295 (505-827-8300).

NEW YORK

New York State Higher Education Services Corporation, 99 Washington Avenue, Albany, NY 12255 (518-473-1574 for federal student loans; 518-474-5642 for state aid).

NORTH CAROLINA

North Carolina State Education Assistance Authority, P.O. Box 2688, Chapel Hill, NC 27515-2688 (919-549-8614).

NORTH DAKOTA

Federal student loans: North Dakota Stafford Loan Agency, c/o Bank of North Dakota, P.O. Box 5509, Bismarck, ND 58502-5509 (701-224-5600).

State aid: Student Financial Assistance Program, North Dakota Board of Higher Education, 10th Floor, State Capitol, Bismarck, ND 58505-0154 (701-224-4114).

OHIO

Federal student loans: Ohio Student Loan Commission, P.O. Box 16610, Columbus, OH 43266-0610 (614-466-3091).

State aid: Student Assistance Office, Ohio Board of Regents, 3600 State Office Tower, 30 East Broad Street, Columbus, OH 43266-0417 (614-466-7420).

OKLAHOMA

Oklahoma State Regents for Higher Education, 500 Education Building, State Capitol Complex, Oklahoma City, OK 73105 (405-521-8262 for federal student loans; 405-525-8180 for state aid).

OREGON

Oregon State Scholarship Commission, 1445 Willamette Street, Eugene, OR 97401-7706 (503-686-3200 for federal student loans; 503-686-4166 for state aid).

PENNSYLVANIA

Pennsylvania Higher Education Assistance Agency, 660 Boas Street, Harrisburg, PA 17102 (in Pennsylvania, 800-692-7392 for federal student loans; 800-692-7435 for state aid).

RHODE ISLAND

Rhode Island Higher Education Assistance Authority, 560 Jefferson Boulevard, Warwick, RI 02886 (401-277-2050).

SOUTH CAROLINA

Federal student loans: South Carolina Student Loan Corporation, Suite 210, Interstate Center, P.O. Box 21487, Columbia, SC 29221 (803-798-0916).

State aid: South Carolina Tuition Grants Commission, 411 Keenan Building, P.O. Box 12159, Columbia, SC 29211 (803-734-1200).

SOUTH DAKOTA

Federal student loans: South Dakota Education Assistance Corporation, 115 First Avenue, SW, Aberdeen, SD 57401 (605-225-6423).

State aid: Department of Education and Cultural Affairs, Richard E. Kniep Building, 700 Governors Drive, Pierre, SD 57501-2293 (605-773-3134).

TENNESSEE

Tennessee Student Assistance Corporation, Suite 1950, Parkway Towers, 404 James Robertson Parkway, Nashville, TN 37219-5097 (615-741-1346; in Tennessee, 800-342-1663).

TEXAS

Federal student loans: Texas Student Loan Corporation, P.O. Box 15996, Austin, TX 78761 (512-835-1900).

State aid: Texas Higher Education Coordinating Board, Texas College and University System, Capitol Station, P.O. Box 12788, Austin, TX 78711 (512-462-6325).

UTAH

Federal student loans: Loan Servicing Corporation of Utah, P.O. Box 30802, Salt Lake City, UT 84130-0802 (801-363-9151).

State aid: Utah State Board of Regents, Suite 550, 3 Triad Center, 355 WN Temple, Salt Lake City, UT 84180-1205 (801-538-5247).

VERMONT

Vermont Student Assistance Corporation, Champlain Mill, P.O. Box 2000, Winooski, VT 05404-2601 (in Vermont, 800-642-9602).

VIRGINIA

Federal student loans: State Education Assistance Authority, Suite 300, 6 North Sixth Street, Richmond, VA 23219 (804-786-2035).

State aid: State Council of Higher Education for Virginia, James Monroe Building, 101 North Fourteenth Street, Richmond, VA 23219 (804-225-2141).

WASHINGTON

Federal student loans: Student Loan Guaranty Association, 500 Colman Building, 811 First Avenue, Seattle, WA 98104 (206-625-1030).

State aid: Higher Education Coordinating Board, 917 Lakeridge Way, GV-11, Olympia, WA 98504.

WEST VIRGINIA

Federal student loans: Higher Education Assistance Foundation, P.O. Box 591, Charleston, WV 25322 (304-345-7211).

State aid: West Virginia Board of Regents, P.O. Box 4007, Charleston, WV 25364 (304-347-1231).

WISCONSIN

Federal student loans: Great Lakes Higher Education Corporation, 2401 International Lane, Madison, WI 53704 (608-246-1800).

State aid: Higher Educational Aids Board, P.O. Box 7885, Madison, WI 53707 (608-267-2206).

WYOMING

Higher Education Assistance Foundation, Suite 320, American National Bank Building, 1912 Capitol Avenue, Cheyenne, WY 82001 (307-635-3259).

Appendix E

Selected Scholarships and Other Awards

This list of scholarships and similar awards was prepared by the Association of American Colleges' Project on the Status and Education of Women. The scholarships are categorized by subject area. The following abbreviations are used when the information is available but does not appear in the program description:

U	Undergraduate students are eligible.
G	Graduate students are eligible.
P	Postdoctoral students are eligible.
FT	Funds can be used for full-time study.
PT	Funds can be used for part-time study.
D	Funds are available only to those in degree programs.
ND	Funds are available for study in nondegree programs.
CC	Funds are available for study in community or junior colleges.
C	Funds are available for study through correspondence courses.
OTT	Funds are available for occupational/technical training.

GENERAL

American Association of University Women Educational Foundation, 2401 Virginia Avenue, NW, Washington, DC 20037. The following awards for those who intend to pursue a professional career in the United States require that an applicant be a U.S. citizen or hold permanent resident status. There are no restrictions on the age of the applicant, the academic field, or the place of study.
- *Dissertation Fellowships.* Awards for women who have successfully completed all required course work and examinations for the doctorate except the defense of their dissertation.
- *Fellowships to American Women in Selected Professions.* Awards to women in their final year of professional training in an M.B.A. program or in the fields of law, medicine, or architecture. Applicants must be students at an accredited U.S. institution.
- *Postdoctoral Fellowships.* Awards for postdoctoral research by those who hold the doctorate at the time of their application.

American Sociological Association Minority Fellowships Program, 1722 N Street, NW, Washington, DC 20036
- *Doctoral Fellowships in Sociology.* Awards are given to qualified black, Hispanic, Native American, and Asian American graduate students who are studying the sociological aspects of mental health issues faced by ethnic and racial minorities. Applicants must be U.S. citizens or residents with a permanent visa.

Business and Professional Women's Foundation, 2012 Massachusetts Avenue, NW, Washington, DC 20036. Both programs described aid mature women who are employed or seeking employment. Applicants for the following awards must be U.S. citizens, be officially accepted into an accredited program or course of study at a U.S. institution, be within twenty-four months of completing their studies, and demonstrate financial need. Applications are available only between July 1 and September 1 and between February 1 and April 1. Deadlines are September 15 and April 15, respectively. FT, PT, D, ND, CC, OTT.
- *Career Advancement Scholarships.* Awarded to women 25 and older.
- *Clairol Loving Care Scholarships.* Awarded to women 30 and older.

Jeanette Rankin Foundation, P.O. Box 4045, Athens, GA 30605. Awards are given to women 35 and older who wish to pursue training or education on the undergraduate level. U, FT, PT, CC, C, OTT.

Soroptimist Training Awards, 1616 Walnut Street, Philadelphia, PA 19103. Awards are given to mature women who, as heads of households, must either enter or return to the job market or further their training to upgrade their employment status. Apply to the local Soroptimist Club. Deadline is December 15.

BUSINESS AND BANKING

American Assembly of Collegiate Schools of Business, Suite 220, 605 Old Ballas Road, St. Louis, MO 63141
- *Doctoral Fellowship in Business Administration.* Provides financial assistance to doctoral students at the dissertation stage who are interested in a career in teaching business administration or management. Application deadline is February 1.
- *National Doctoral Fellowship Program in Business and Management.* Provides financial assistance to first-year doctoral students in business who are interested in pursuing a business-faculty career. Graduates in nonbusiness disciplines are also encouraged to apply. Deadline is January 1.

Business and Professional Women's Foundation, 2012 Massachusetts Avenue, NW, Washington, DC 20036
- *Avon Products Foundation Scholarships for Careers in Sales.* Awarded to women who head households and are supporting one or more dependents while taking courses leading to careers in sales. Applicants must be 25 or older.
- *The BPW/Sears Roebuck Loan Fund for Women in Graduate Business Studies.* Loans are available to women seeking a master's degree in business administration. Applicants must be U.S. citizens, have written notice of acceptance at a school accredited by the

American Assembly of Collegiate Schools of Business, and demonstrate financial need. Study may be full- or part-time. Applications are available after February 1 and are due May 1.

HUMANITIES AND THE ARTS

The Bunting Institute, Radcliffe College, 34 Concord Avenue, Cambridge, MA 02138
- *The Bunting Fellowship Program.* These fellowships provide support for women to pursue independent research or to work in academic or professional fields, in creative writing, or in the arts. Applicants should have received their doctorates at least two years prior to the date of fellowship appointment. Applicants in creative writing, the visual arts, or music are expected to be at an equivalent stage in their professional development.

The D'Arcy McNickle Center for the History of the American Indian, Newberry Library, 60 West Walton Street, Chicago, IL 60610
- *Francis C. Allen Fellowships.* Fellowships are available to women of Native American heritage who are pursuing an academic program beyond their undergraduate degree. Stipends cover travel and living expenses. Applications are due February 1 or August 1.

Woodrow Wilson National Fellowship Foundation, 16 John Street, P.O. Box 288, Princeton, NJ 08542
- *Mellon Fellowships in the Humanities.* One hundred to 125 awards are given to college seniors or recent graduates to begin graduate work toward a career of teaching and scholarship in the humanities. Candidates must be U.S. citizens, show evidence of outstanding promise, and be nominated by a faculty member. Awards may be renewed for up to three years.

LAW

Mexican American Legal Defense and Education Fund, 11th Floor, 634 South Spring Street, Los Angeles, CA 90014
- *Law School Scholarship Program.* Assistance to Hispanic law students who demonstrate financial need. Any person of Hispanic descent who is enrolled or will be enrolled as a full-time law student is eligible to apply. Deadline is May 30.

NAACP Legal Defense and Education Fund, Suite 1600, 99 Hudson Street, New York, NY 10013
- *Earl Warren Legal Training Program, Inc.* Grants to black students entering law school, preferably in the South. Deadline is March 15.

MEDICINE AND HEALTH

American Fund for Dental Health, Suite 820, 211 East Chicago Avenue, Chicago, IL 60611. The following scholarships are available to U.S. citizens enrolled or accepted at dental schools or dental laboratory technology programs accredited by the American Dental Association.
- *Minority Dental Student Scholarships.* Available to black, Hispanic, and Native American students for the first year of study. Upon student's reapplication, scholarship may be renewed for a second year.

155

- *Scholarships in Dental Laboratory Technology.* Available for tuition and education-related costs for one year of study. Upon student's reapplication, scholarship may be renewed for a second year.

American Medical Women's Association Medical Education Loan Program, 465 Grand Avenue, New York, NY 10002. Assistance to women in their first, second, or third year of medical school. Applicants must be U.S. citizens attending a U.S. institution full-time.

Business and Professional Women's Foundation, 2012 Massachusetts Avenue, NW, Washington, DC 20036

- *New York Life Foundation Scholarship for Women in the Health Professions.* Assists women 25 and older to enter or advance within the health-care professions. Applicants must be U.S. citizens and be within twenty-four months of completing an accredited program at a U.S. institution. The scholarships cover academic, vocational, and paraprofessional courses. Applications are available only from February 1 to April 1 and from July 1 to September 1. Deadlines are April 15 and September 15. U, FT, PT, D, ND, CC, OTT.

Indian Health Employees Scholarship Fund, Room 215, Federal Building, Aberdeen, SD 57401. Supports students of Native American descent who are entering health-related fields. Priority is given to students from North Dakota, South Dakota, and Minnesota. U, FT, PT.

National Society of the Daughters of the American Revolution (DAR), Office of the Committees, 1776 D Street, NW, Washington, DC 20006. State DAR organizations and local DAR chapters have their own scholarship programs. Contact the national office or the chair of your state's scholarship committee for information. The following medical scholarships are administered by the national society. No affiliation with the DAR is required.

- *The Caroline E. Holt Educational Fund Scholarships.* Available to women currently studying in an accredited nursing program or about to enter an accredited institution in the next semester.
- *Occupational Therapy Scholarships.* Available to those who are studying or have been accepted to study physical, music, or art therapy.

U.S. Department of Health and Human Services, Student and Institutional Assistance Branch, Division of Student Assistance, Room 8-38, Parklawn Building, Rockville, MD 20857. Offers loans and scholarships to assist students in the medical field. Applicants must be U.S. citizens or permanent residents. College financial aid offices can provide additional information and applications.

- *Health Professions Student Loan Program.* Provides long-term, low-interest loans to students preparing to become physicians, dentists, osteopaths, optometrists, pharmacists, podiatrists, or veterinarians. Applicants must be enrolled or accepted for enrollment full-time.
- *Nursing Student Loan Program.* Makes long-term, low-interest loans available to nursing students. Applicants must be enrolled as full- or half-time students in a program leading to a diploma, an associate degree, a bachelor's degree, or a graduate degree in nursing.
- *Program of Financial Assistance for Disadvantaged Health Professions Students.* Offers assistance with no service or financial obliga-

tion to disadvantaged health professions students of exceptional financial need who wish to pursue a career in medicine, osteopathic medicine, or dentistry.

- *Scholarship Program for First-Year Students of Exceptional Financial Need.* Provides scholarships free of service or financial obligation to exceptionally needy students who wish to pursue a career in medicine, dentistry, optometry, podiatry, pharmacy, or veterinary medicine. Applicants must be enrolled or accepted for enrollment as full-time students in a health professions school.

SCIENCE AND ENGINEERING

American Geophysical Union, Member Programs Division, 2700 Florida Avenue, NW, Washington, DC 20009

- *The June Bacon-Bercey Scholarship.* A $500 scholarship for a female student of atmospheric sciences. Eligibility is based on academic achievement and promise and is limited to one of the following: a first-year graduate student in a degree-granting program in atmospheric sciences, an undergraduate in atmospheric sciences who has been accepted into a graduate program in atmospheric sciences, or a student in a two-year institution who has earned at least 6 hours of credit toward her degree and has been accepted into a Bachelor of Science program. Application deadline is April 15.

Business and Professional Women's Foundation, 2012 Massachusetts Avenue, NW, Washington, DC 20036

- *The BPW Foundation Loan Fund for Women in Engineering Studies.* Assists women in their final two years of any accredited engineering program, including undergraduate, refresher, and conversion programs, as well as graduate studies. Study may be full- or part-time (at least 6 semester hours or the equivalent). Applicants must be U.S. citizens, have written notice of acceptance to a course of study in engineering that is accredited by the Accreditation Board for Engineering and Technology, and demonstrate financial need. Applications are available from February 1 through April 15. Deadline is May 1.

Graduate Engineering for Minorities (GEM), National Consortium for Graduate Degrees for Minorities, Inc., Box 537, Notre Dame, IN 46556. Provides for full-time master's-level study in engineering and paid summer internship opportunities for Native American, black, Mexican American, and Puerto Rican students. Applicants must be U.S. citizens and must plan to attend a GEM member school.

Iota Sigma Pi, c/o Dr. Linda Munchausen, Department of Chemistry and Physics, Box 372, Southeastern Louisiana University, Hammond, LA 70402

- *The Gladys Anderson Emerson Undergraduate Scholarship.* Awarded to women undergraduates in either a chemistry or biochemistry curriculum at an accredited institution. Applicants must be full-time students and have at least one semester of chemistry left to complete. Application deadline is January 1.

National Chicano Council on Higher Education, Science Fellowship Program, School of Biological Sciences, T40, University of California, Irvine, CA 92717

- *Undergraduate Science Fellowships for Hispanics and Chicanos.* Supports approximately twenty undergraduate students who are interested in pursuing a doctorate and an academic career in one of the council's designated scientific fields. Applicants must be Hispanic or Chicano and be either sophomores or juniors enrolled in a U.S. university or college. Application deadline is November 16.

Society of Women Engineers Scholarship Program, Room 305, United Engineering Center, 345 East 47th Street, New York, NY 10017. Administers approximately thirty-eight scholarships annually, varying from $500 to $2500. The awards are granted to women at all levels of undergraduate and graduate study. Some are available specifically to reentry women. Applicants must be attending a school, college, or university with an accredited engineering program. Requests for information must be accompanied by an SASE.

Zonta International, 557 West Randolph Street, Chicago, IL 60606
- *Zonta Amelia Earhart Fellowships.* Awards made to women qualified for graduate study in aerospace-related sciences and engineering. Applications are due January 1.

WOMEN'S ISSUES

Business and Professional Women's Foundation, 2012 Massachusetts Avenue, NW, Washington, DC 20036
- *Lena Lake Forrest Fellowships and BPW Foundation Research Grants.* Supports contemporary and historical studies that provide perspectives on economic issues of importance to today's working women. Applicants must be U.S. citizens and generally must be doctoral candidates or postdoctoral scholars. However, others may apply if they demonstrate that their proposed research will be conducted under standards of scholarship recognized at the doctoral level. Applicants are required to write a preliminary letter requesting an application form and to include a concise statement about their proposed research subject and academic qualifications. Applications are available from September 1 until December 15 and must be postmarked on or before January 1.

Center for Women in Government, Draper 302, State University of New York at Albany, 1400 Washington Avenue, Albany, NY 12222
- *Fellowships on Women and Public Policy.* Enables graduate students to develop public policy specialties concerning women. Applicants must have completed 12 graduate credits at a college or university located in New York State. Applications are due end of May.

Douglass College, Voorhees Chapel, New Brunswick, NJ 08903
- *Junior Year at Douglass Program in Women's Studies.* Provides an opportunity for undergraduates to spend a semester or a year at Douglass College focusing on women's studies. U, FT, D.

Mary Lizzie Saunders Clapp Fund and Radcliffe Research Resource Awards, Schlesinger Library, Radcliffe College, 10 Garden Street, Cambridge, MA 02138. Small grants cover the cost of travel and other expenses related to pursuing research at the Arthur and Elizabeth Schlesinger Library on the History of Women in America.

National Women's Studies Association (NWSA), c/o Caryn McTighe Musil, Director, University of Maryland, College Park, MD 20742
- *Naiad-NWSA Graduate Scholarship in Lesbian Studies.* Awarded to a student doing research for or writing a master's thesis or doctoral dissertation in lesbian studies. Applicants need not be enrolled in a women's studies program. Preference will be given to candidates who are NWSA members.
- *Pergamon-NWSA Graduate Scholarships in Women's Studies.* Two scholarships are awarded to students doing research for or writing a master's thesis or doctoral dissertation in women's studies. Applicants need not be enrolled in a women's studies program. Preference will be given to candidates who are NWSA members and whose research project has relevance to class issues, women of color, or Third-World women. Application deadline is March 1.

Women's Research and Education Institute, Suite 400, 1700 18th Street, NW, Washington, DC 20009
- *Congressional Fellowships on Women and Public Policy.* Awards provide for students to work for one academic year for a member of Congress or congressional committee staff on policy issues affecting women. All students in graduate or preprofessional programs in the United States are eligible. About ten fellowships are available each year.

Woodrow Wilson National Fellowship Foundation, Department WS, Box 642, Princeton, NJ 08542
- *Woodrow Wilson Women's Studies Research Grants for Doctoral Candidates.* Grants for research expenses are designed to encourage original and significant research about women. Applicants may be enrolled in doctoral programs in any field of study but must have completed all predissertation requirements in any field of study at a graduate school in the United States.

Appendix F

Books About Financial Aid

Many of the following books can be found in community or campus libraries, as well as at the offices of university counselors and financial aid officers.

Better Late Than Never; Financial Aid for Reentry Women Seeking Education and Training. Washington, D.C.: Women's Equity Action League. Directory of more than fifty sources of financial aid for women returning to school, updating their credentials, or changing careers.

Betterton, Don M. *How the Military Will Help You Pay for College.* Princeton, N.J.: Peterson's Guides, 1990. A detailed discussion of the major military-based sources of tuition aid, including scholarships, tuition-payment programs, and ROTC.

———. *How to Pay for College.* Princeton, N.J.: Peterson's Guides. Revised annually. Pamphlet giving step-by-step guidance.

Chronicle Four-Year College Databook. Moravia, N.Y.: Chronicle Guidance Publications. Revised annually. Information on scholarships at four-year colleges and universities throughout the United States.

Chronicle Student Aid Annual. Moravia, N.Y.: Chronicle Guidance Publications. Revised annually. Information on approximately 1,350 financial aid programs for undergraduate, graduate, and postgraduate study. Includes programs offered by private organizations and foundations, national and international labor unions, and federal and state agencies.

Chronicle Two-Year College Databook. Moravia, N.Y.: Chronicle Guidance Publications. Revised annually. Describes scholarships offered by two-year colleges throughout the United States.

Cole, Katherine W., ed. *Minority Organizations: A National Directory.* Garrett Park, Md.: Garrett Park Press, 1987. Lists more than 7,100 minority membership organizations and programs developed by other organizations to serve minority-group members.

The College Blue Book: Scholarships, Fellowships, Grants, and Loans, 21st ed. Riverside, N.J.: Macmillan, 1987. Comprehensive list of public and private financial aid sources at every level of study. Includes a section on women and minorities.

Dineen, Patricia. *Opportunities for Research and Study.* New York: National Council for Research on Women. Revised annually. Lists fellowships, affiliated-scholar programs, grants, and internships sponsored by the council's member centers.

A Directory of Federal Research and Development Agencies' Programs to Attract Women, Minorities, and the Physically Handicapped to Careers in Science and Engineering. Washington, D.C.: National Science Foundation. Lists the agency, name of the program, person to contact, eligibility requirements, deadlines, and number of awards. Free from National Science Foundation, 1800 G Street, NW, Washington, D.C. 20550 (ask for NSF 85-51).

Earn and Learn, Cooperative Education Opportunities Offered by the Federal Government: Sponsors, Occupational Fields, and Participating Colleges. Alexandria, Va.: Octameron Press. Revised annually. Lists cooperative education opportunities at more than 850 colleges. Also contains suggestions on ways for students to earn money and then turn their jobs into professional employment.

Foundation Grants to Individuals. New York: The Foundation Center, 1986. Describes more than 950 foundations that offer scholarships to undergraduates and graduate students.

Goeller, Priscilla S. *The A's and B's of Academic Scholarships.* Alexandria, Va.: Octameron Press. Revised annually. Describes more than 100,000 scholarships for students with ACT scores higher than 20.

Grants at a Glance. Washington, D.C.: Association for Women in Science, 1987. A list of more than 350 awards, fellowships, and grants for students and professionals in engineering and the life sciences, physical sciences, and social sciences.

Institute of International Education. *Financial Resources for International Study.* Princeton, N.J.: Peterson's Guides, 1989. Describes over 500 grants of at least $500 for undergraduate, graduate, and postgraduate students, as well as working professionals, who wish to study abroad.

Leider, Anna, and Robert Leider. *Don't Miss Out: The Ambitious Student's Guide to Financial Aid.* Alexandria, Va.: Octameron Press. Revised annually. Complete description of all major federal, state, and private student-aid programs. There are special sections on women, minorities, and the disabled.

Need a Lift? Indianapolis: The American Legion. Revised annually. Primarily for undergraduates, contains sources of career, scholarship, and loan information, as well as sources of aid for children of veterans. It also describes state laws that provide for educational benefits.

Peterson's College Money Handbook. Princeton, N.J.: Peterson's Guides. Revised annually. Gives a full account of costs and financial aid at more than 1,700 accredited four-year colleges in the United States.

Peterson's Financial Aid Service. Princeton, N.J.: Peterson's Guides. Revised annually. Software that helps users to determine their financial need, to compare costs at different types of colleges, to predict their chances of receiving the aid they need at specific colleges, and to pinpoint scholarships for which they may be eligible.

Peterson's Grants for Graduate Students, 2nd ed. Princeton, N.J.: Peterson's Guides, 1989. Comprehensive information on grants and fellowships exclusively for graduate students, including where to look and how to increase your chances of winning.

Peterson's State and Federal Aid Programs for College Students. Princeton, N.J.: Peterson's Guides. Revised annually. State-by-state description of aid programs, with eligibility information, application dates and procedures, and addresses.

Schlachter, Gail Ann. *Directory of Financial Aids for Minorities.* Redwood City, Calif.: Reference Service Press. Revised biennially. Lists over

1,000 financial aid programs designed primarily or exclusively for Asians, blacks, Hispanics, and Native Americans. Also has a list of state resources and a bibliography of financial aid directories.

———. *Directory of Financial Aids for Women.* Redwood City, Calif.: Reference Service Press. Revised biennially. A listing of over 1,500 scholarships, fellowships, loans, grants, internships, awards, and prizes available to women. Also includes a list of state resources and a bibliography of financial aid directories.

Appendix G

Regional Offices of the Women's Bureau

Region I *(Connecticut, Maine, Massachusetts, New Hampshire, Rhode Island, Vermont)*
JFK Building, Room 1600
Boston, MA 02203
Telephone: 617-565-1988

Region II *(New Jersey, New York, Puerto Rico, Virgin Islands)*
1515 Broadway, Room 3575
New York, NY 10036
Telephone: 212-944-3445

Region III *(Delaware, District of Columbia, Maryland, Pennsylvania, Virginia, West Virginia)*
3535 Market Street, Room 13280
Philadelphia, PA 19104
Telephone: 215-596-1183

Region IV *(Alabama, Florida, Georgia, Kentucky, Mississippi, North and South Carolina, Tennessee)*
1371 Peachtree Street, NE, Room 323
Atlanta, GA 30367
Telephone: 404-881-4461

Region V *(Illinois, Indiana, Michigan, Minnesota, Ohio, Wisconsin)*
230 South Dearborn Street, 10th Floor
Chicago, IL 60604
Telephone: 312-353-6985

Region VI *(Arkansas, Louisiana, New Mexico, Oklahoma, Texas)*
555 Griffin Square Building, Room 731
Dallas, TX 75202
Telephone: 214-767-6985

Region VII *(Iowa, Kansas, Missouri, Nebraska)*
911 Walnut Street, Room 2511
Kansas City, MO 64106
Telephone: 816-374-6108

Region VIII *(Colorado, Montana, North and South Dakota, Utah, Wyoming)*
1961 Stout Street, Room 1456
Denver, CO 80202
Telephone: 303-844-4138

Region IX *(Arizona, California, Hawaii, Nevada)*
Federal Building, Room 9301
450 Golden Gate Avenue
San Francisco, CA 94102
Telephone: 415-556-2377

Region X *(Alaska, Idaho, Oregon, Washington)*
Federal Building, Room 3094
909 First Avenue
Seattle, WA 98174
Telephone: 206-442-1534

MORE OUTSTANDING TITLES FROM PETERSON'S

DEGREES OF SUCCESS

Pam Mendelsohn

In recent years, an increasing number of women have begun adding a student role to their already busy lives. *Degrees of Success* is filled with the true stories of such women. It is an insightful and compelling book that examines the *long-range* effects of reentering student life.

Included are profiles of ordinary women who have done extraordinary things. In their own words, these women describe how their careers, their family lives, their life-styles, and their self-images have shifted.

$10.95 paperback

PETERSON'S GUIDE TO FOUR-YEAR COLLEGES 1991

Profiling 1,950 accredited institutions that grant baccalaureate degrees in the United States and Canada, this guide includes the highest-quality and most accurate data on everything from admission requirements to campus life.

More than 800 In-Depth Descriptions of the Colleges—not found in any other college guide—go beyond the data profiles to provide a full, personal look at each college.

Also included are college directories—on over 450 majors as well as cost, entrance difficulty, and geographic area.

$17.95 paperback

PETERSON'S GUIDE TO TWO-YEAR COLLEGES 1991

The leader among two-year guides, this is the most complete and accurate source of information on every accredited institution in the United States that grants the associate degree as its highest degree—1,494 colleges in all. The guide includes:

- Concise statistical profiles on every college
- Two-page In-Depth Descriptions of the Colleges, which give a balanced and complete picture of the college

$13.95 paperback

Peterson's Annual Guides to Graduate Study
Complete Coverage of More Than 31,000 Graduate and Professional Programs in the U.S. and Canada

---

PETERSON'S GUIDE TO GRADUATE AND PROFESSIONAL PROGRAMS: AN OVERVIEW 1991
$20.95 paperback

PETERSON'S GUIDE TO GRADUATE PROGRAMS IN THE HUMANITIES AND SOCIAL SCIENCES 1991
$32.95 paperback

PETERSON'S GUIDE TO GRADUATE PROGRAMS IN THE BIOLOGICAL AND AGRICULTURAL SCIENCES 1991
$38.95 paperback

PETERSON'S GUIDE TO GRADUATE PROGRAMS IN BUSINESS, EDUCATION, HEALTH, AND LAW 1991
$20.95 paperback

PETERSON'S GUIDE TO GRADUATE PROGRAMS IN THE PHYSICAL SCIENCES AND MATHEMATICS 1991
$28.95 paperback

PETERSON'S GUIDE TO GRADUATE PROGRAMS IN ENGINEERING AND APPLIED SCIENCES 1991
$32.95 paperback

Look for these and other Peterson's titles in your local bookstore